YOUR TOTAL SOLUTION FOR MATH

GRADE 2

An imprint of Carson-Dellosa Publishing LLC
P.O. Box 35665
Greensboro, NC 27425 USA

Brighter Child®
An imprint of Carson-Dellosa Publishing, LLC
P.O. Box 35665
Greensboro, NC 27425-5665

carsondellosa.com

ISBN 978-1-4838-0711-9

01-097147811

Table of Contents

Name _____

Dapper Dog's Campout

Directions: Dapper Dog is going on a camping trip. Draw an **X** on the word in each row that does not belong.

1. flashlight   candle   radio   fire

2. shirt   pants   coat   bat

3. cow   car   bus   train

4. beans   hot dog   ball   bread

5. gloves   hat   book   boots

6. fork   butter   cup   plate

7. book   ball   bat   milk

8. dogs   bees   flies   ants

Your Total Solution for Math: Grade 2

Classification Fun

Directions: Write each word in the correct row at the bottom of the page.

car   pencil   chalk   radio   boat   fork

plate   friend   airplane   drum   spoon   crayon

Things we ride in:

_____   _____   _____

Things we eat with:

_____   _____   _____

Things we draw with:

_____   _____   _____

Things we listen to:

_____   _____   _____

Name _____

Where Does It Belong?

Directions: Read the words in the fish tank. Write each word in its correct place.

Joe   cat   blue   Tim

two   dog   red   ten

Sue   green   pig   six

Name
Words   _____   _____   _____

Number
Words   _____   _____   _____

Animal
Words   _____   _____   _____

Color
Words   _____   _____   _____

Classifying

Directions: The words in each list form a group. Choose the word from the box that describes each group and write it on the line.

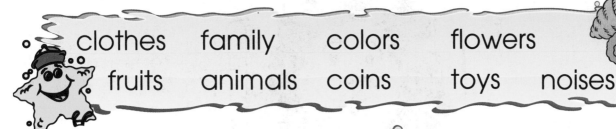

clothes   family   colors   flowers

fruits   animals   coins   toys   noises

rose	crash 	mother
buttercup	bang	father
tulip	ring	sister
daisy	pop	brother
_____	_____	_____

puzzle	green	grapes
wagon	purple	orange
blocks	blue	apple
doll	red	plum
_____	_____	_____

shirt	dime 	dog
socks	penny	horse
dress	nickel	elephant
coat	quarter	moose
_____	_____	_____

Name _____

Classifying: Foods

Darcy likes fruit and things made from fruit. She also likes bread.

Directions: Circle the things on the menu that Darcy will eat.

MENU

apple pie   corn
peas   rolls
beans   banana bread
oranges   grape drink
chicken

Your Total Solution for Math: Grade 2

Classifying: Animal Habitats

Directions: Read the story. Then, write each animal's name under **WATER** or **LAND** to tell where it lives.

Animals live in different habitats. A **habitat** is the place of an animal's natural home. Many animals live on land and others live in water. Most animals that live in water breathe with gills. Animals that live on land breathe with lungs.

fish	shrimp	giraffe	dog
cat	eel	whale	horse
bear	deer	shark	jellyfish

WATER

1._____   4._____

2._____   5._____

3._____   6._____

LAND

1._____   4._____

2._____   5._____

3._____   6._____

Happy Hikers

Directions: Trace a path through the maze by counting from 1 to 10 in the correct order. Color the picture.

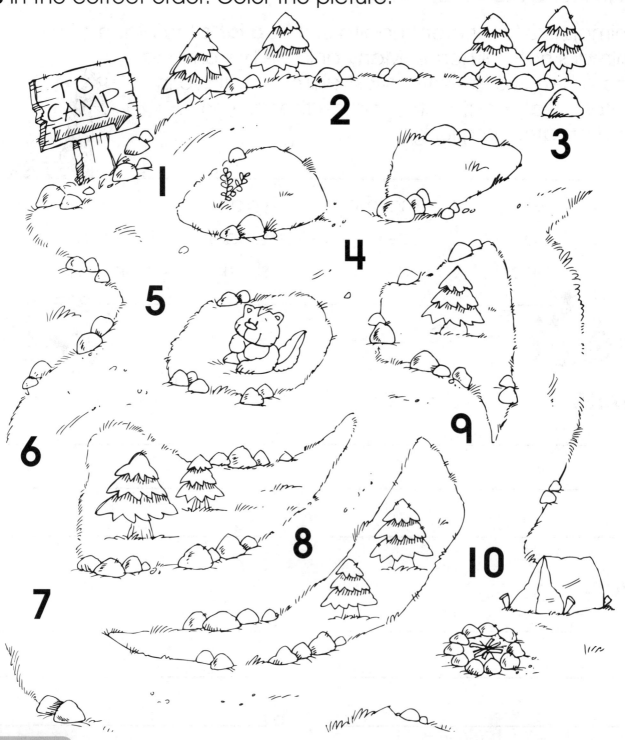

Your Total Solution for Math: Grade 2

Zany Zoo

Directions: Count and color each group of animals. Cut out the numbers and glue them in the correct boxes.

3	5	1	2	4

Rainbow-Colored Numbers

Directions: Color the spaces: **1 = red**, **2 = blue**, **3 = yellow**,
4 = green, and **5 = orange**.

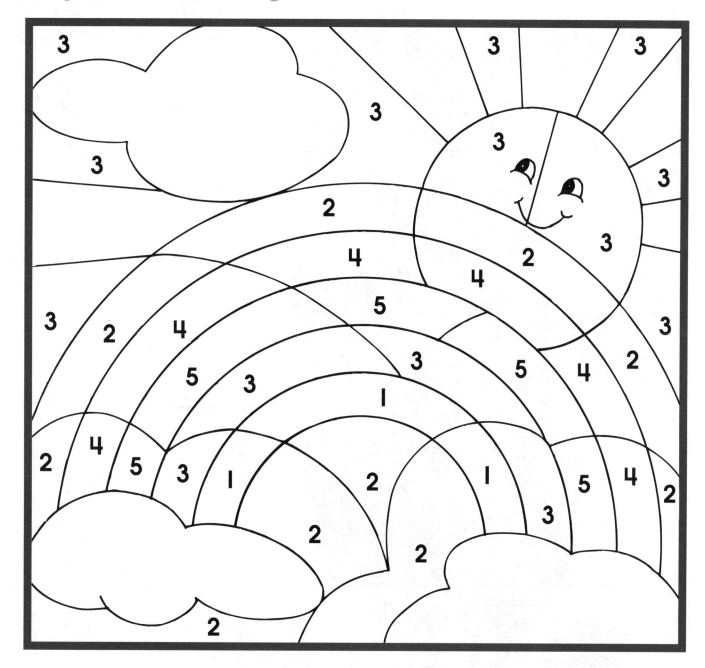

Name _____

Clown Capers

Directions: Count the number of each thing in the picture. Write the number on the line.

Your Total Solution for Math: Grade 2

Name _____

Take an Animal Count!

Directions: Count each group of zoo animals. Draw a line from the number to the correct number word. The first one shows you what to do.

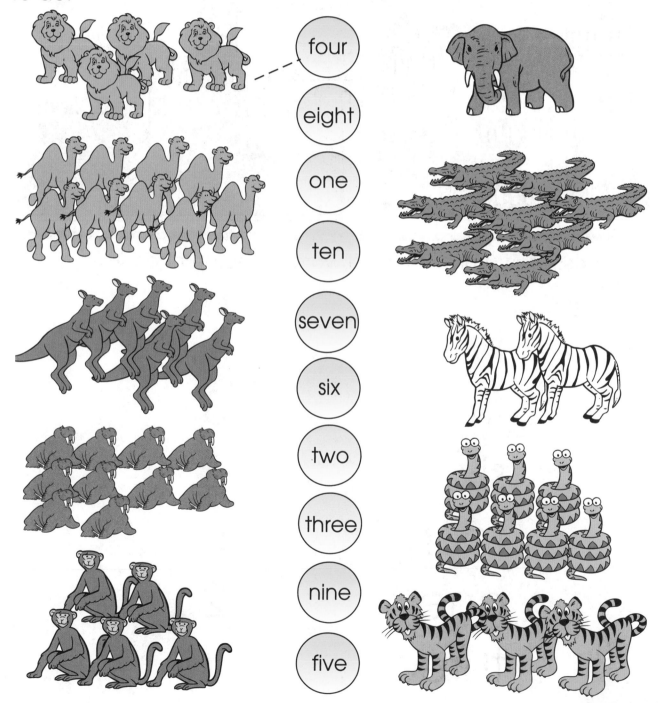

four

eight

one

ten

seven

six

two

three

nine

five

Name _____

Number Words

Directions: Number the buildings from one to six.

Directions: Draw a line from the word to the number.

two	1
five	3
six	5
four	6
one	2
three	4

Your Total Solution for Math: Grade 2

Name _____

Number Words

Directions: Number the buildings from five to ten.

Directions: Draw a line from the word to the number.

nine	8
seven	10
five	7
eight	5
six	9
ten	6

   Name _____

Sequencing Numbers

Sequencing is putting numbers in the correct order.

Directions: Write the missing numbers.

Example: 4, __5__ , 6

3, _____ , 5   7, _____ , 9   8, _____ , 10

6, _____ , 8   _____ , 3, 4   _____ , 5, 6

5, 6, _____   _____ , 6, 7   _____ , 3, 4

_____ , 9, 10   _____ , 7, 8   2, _____ , 4

2, 3, _____   1, 2, _____   7, 8, _____

2, _____ , 4   _____ , 7, 8   4, _____ , 6

6, 7, _____   2, 3, _____   1, _____ , 3

7, 8, _____   _____ , 3, 4   _____ , 9, 10

                  Your Total Solution for Math: Grade 2

Counting

Directions: Write the numbers that are:

next in order	one less	one greater
22, 23, ____ , ____	____ , 16	6, ____
674, ____ , ____	____ , 247	125, ____
227, ____ , ____	____ , 550	499, ____
199, ____ , ____	____ , 333	750, ____
329, ____ , ____	____ , 862	933, ____

Directions: Write the missing numbers.

Name _____

Note the Count

Directions: Count the number of notes on each page of music. Write the number on the line below it. In each box, circle the greater number of notes.

Directions: Color the note in each box that is greater.

     Your Total Solution for Math: Grade 2

Teddy Bears in a Row

Directions: Cut out the bears at the bottom of the page. Glue them where they belong in number order.

Plump Piglets

Directions: Read the clues to find out how many ears of corn each pig ate. Write the number on the line below each pig.

I ate the number that comes before **26**.

I ate the number that comes between **87** and **89**.

I ate the number that comes after **92**.

Patsy

Horace

Pinky

I ate the number that comes before **57**.

Hilda

I ate the number that comes between **39** and **41**.

Porky

Who ate the most? _____   Who ate the least? _____

Name _____

Counting by Twos

Directions: Count by 2s to draw the path to the store.

Your Total Solution for Math: Grade 2

Name _____

Two for the Pool

Directions: Count by **2**s. Write the numbers to **30** in the water drops. Begin at the top of the slide and go down.

Name _____

Counting by Fives

Directions: Count by **5**s to draw the path to the playground.

     Your Total Solution for Math: Grade 2

Name _____

Cookie Clues

Directions: Find out what holds something good! Count by **5**s to connect the dots. Color the picture.

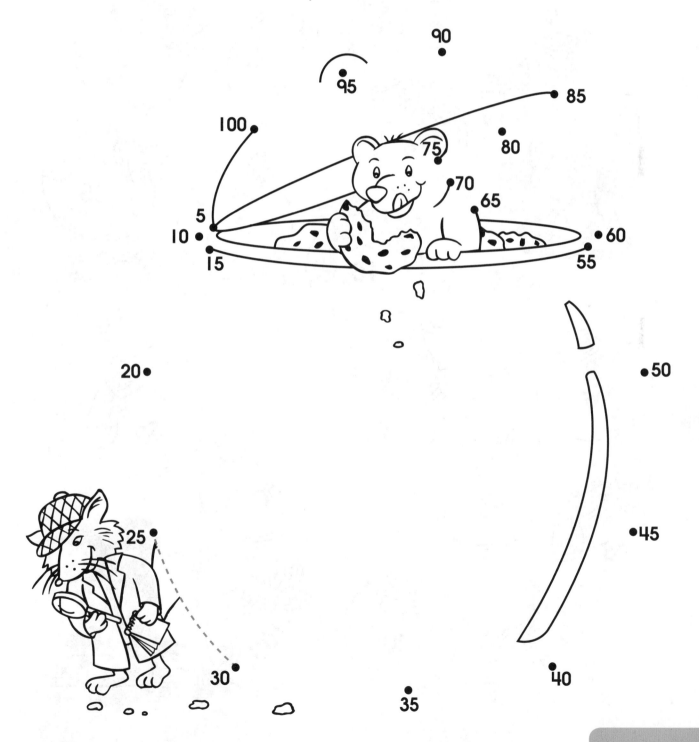

Name _____

Desert Trek

Directions: Count by **10**s. Color each canteen with a **10** to lead the camel to the watering hole.

Your Total Solution for Math: Grade 2

Caterpillar Count

Directions: Count by **5**s.
Draw a triangle around each number as you count by **5**s.

1	2	3	4	5	6	7	8	9	10
11	12	13	14	15	16	17	18	19	20
21	22	23	24	25	26	27	28	29	30
31	32	33	34	35	36	37	38	39	40
41	42	43	44	45	46	47	48	49	50

Directions: Count by **5**s.

5   10   ___   ___   ___   ___   ___

___   ___

Directions: Count by **10**s.
Draw a box around each number as you count by **10**s.

1	2	3	4	5	6	7	8	9	10
11	12	13	14	15	16	17	18	19	20
21	22	23	24	25	26	27	28	29	30
31	32	33	34	35	36	37	38	39	40
41	42	43	44	45	46	47	48	49	50

Directions: Count by **10**s.   10   ___   ___   ___   ___

Name _____

Name _____

Counting by Twos, Fives, and Tens

Directions: Write the missing numbers.

Count by **2**s.

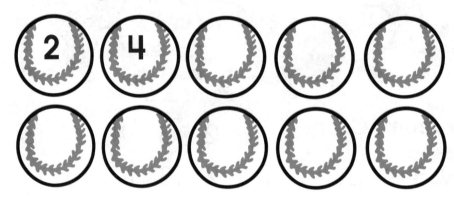

Count by **5**s.

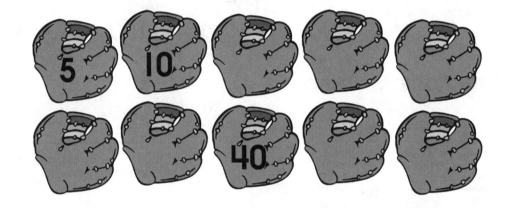

Count by **10**s.

Your Total Solution for Math: Grade 2

Critter Count

Directions: Count by **2**s, **5**s, and **10**s to find the "critter count."

Each worm = 2. Count by **2**s to find the total.

 = _____

 = _____

Each turtle = 5. Count by **5**s to find the total.

= _____

= _____

Each ladybug = 10. Count by **10**s to find the total.

= _____

= _____

Name _____

Hundred Chart

Directions: Count to 100.

1	2	3	4	5	6	7	8	9	10
11	12	13	14	15	16	17	18	19	20
21	22	23	24	25	26	27	28	29	30
31	32	33	34	35	36	37	38	39	40
41	42	43	44	45	46	47	48	49	50
51	52	53	54	55	56	57	58	59	60
61	62	63	64	65	66	67	68	69	70
71	72	73	74	75	76	77	78	79	80
81	82	83	84	85	86	87	88	89	90
91	92	93	94	95	96	97	98	99	100

Largest and Smallest

Directions: In each shape, circle the smallest number. Draw a square around the largest number.

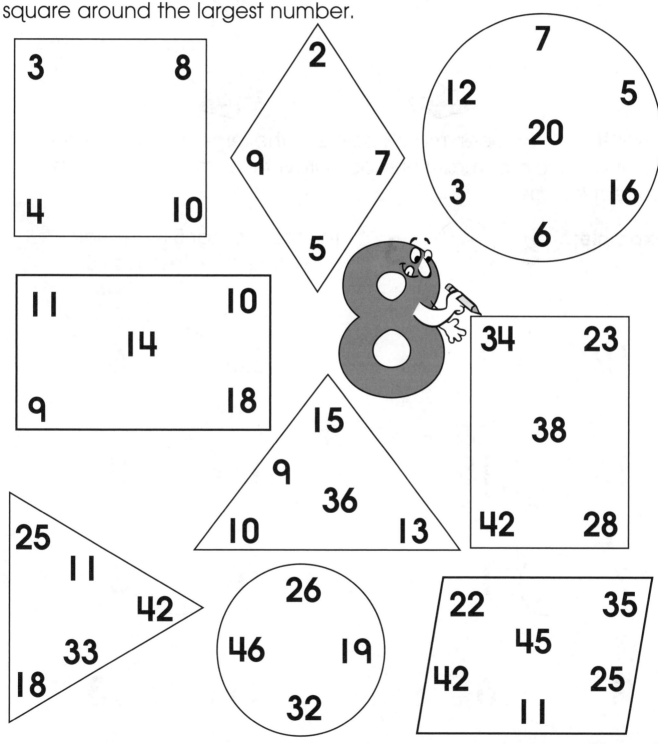

Name _____

Less Than, Greater Than

Directions: The open mouth points to the larger number. The small point goes to the smaller number. Draw the symbol < or > to the correct number.

Example: 5 3   This means that 5 is greater than 3, and 3 is less than 5.

12 ◯ 2   16 ◯ 6

16 ◯ 15   1 ◯ 2

7 ◯ 1   19 ◯ 5

9 ◯ 6   11 ◯ 13

Fishing for Answers

5 > 3
5 is greater than 3

3 < 5
3 is less than 5

Directions: Write the missing numbers in the number line.

1	2				6				

3 > 2

3 < 4

Directions: Write > or <. Use the number line to help you.

5 ◯ 2	1 ◯ 7	1 ◯ 9	8 ◯ 5
3 ◯ 4	9 ◯ 3	8 ◯ 7	2 ◯ 4
6 ◯ 5	5 ◯ 3	5 ◯ 7	3 ◯ 5
7 ◯ 3	7 ◯ 6	2 ◯ 8	4 ◯ 2

Name _____

Who Has the Most?

Directions: Circle the correct answer.

1. Traci has 3 s.
   Bob has 4 s.
   Bill has 5 s.
   Who has the most s?
   Traci   Bob   Bill

2. Pam has 7 s.
   Joe has 5 s.
   Jane has 6 s.
   Who has the most s?
   Pam   Joe   Jane

3. Jennifer has 23 s.
   Sandy has 19 s.
   Jack has 25 s.
   Who has the most s?
   Jennifer   Sandy   Jack

4. Ali has 19 s.
   Burt has 18 s.
   Brent has 17 s.
   Who has the most s?
   Ali   Burt   Brent

5. The boys have 14 s.
   The girls have 16 s.
   The teachers have 17 s.
   Who has the most s?
   boys   girls   teachers

6. Rose has 12 s.
   Betsy has 11 s.
   Leslie has 13 s.
   Who has the most s?
   Rose   Betsy   Leslie

© Carson-Dellosa • CD-704555
Your Total Solution for Math: Grade 2

Who Has the Fewest?

Directions: Circle the correct answer.

1. Pat had 4 s.

   Charles had 3 s.

   Andrea had 5 s.

   Who had the fewest number

   of s?

   Pat   Charles   Andrea

2. Jeff has 5 🏀s.

   John has 4 🏀s.

   Bill has 6 🏀s.

   Who has the fewest number

   of 🏀s?

   Jeff   John   Bill

3. Jane has 7 ⚾s.

   Susan has 9 ⚾s.

   Fred has 8 ⚾s.

   Who has the fewest number

   of ⚾s?

   Jane   Susan   Fred

4. Charles bought 12 🏐 s.

   Rose bought 6 🏐 s.

   Dawn bought 24 🏐 s.

   Who bought the fewest

   number of 🏐 s?

   Charles   Rose   Dawn

5. John had 9 🏈 s.

   Jack had 8 🏈 s.

   Mark had 7 🏈 s.

   Who had the fewest

   number of 🏈 s?

   John   Jack   Mark

6. Edith bought 12 ⚾ s.

   Michelle bought 16 ⚾ s.

   Marty bought 13 ⚾s.

   Who bought the fewest

   number of ⚾s?

   Edith   Michelle   Marty

Name _____

Orderly Ordinals

Directions: Write each word on the correct line to put the words in order.

second	fifth	seventh	first	tenth
third	eighth	sixth	fourth	ninth

1. _____

2. _____

3. _____

4. _____

5. _____

6. _____

7. _____

8. _____

9. _____

10. _____

Directions: Which picture is circled in each row? Underline the word that tells the correct number.

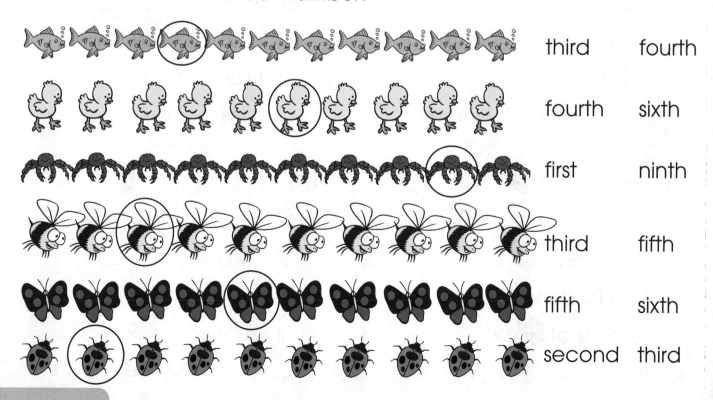

third   fourth

fourth   sixth

first   ninth

third   fifth

fifth   sixth

second   third

Your Total Solution for Math: Grade 2

Name _____

Which Place in the Race?

Directions: Write the correct word to tell each runner's place in the race.

first   second   third   fourth   fifth   sixth   seventh

_____

_____

_____

_____

_____

_____

_____

_____

Name _____

Flags First

Directions:

Color the ninth flag **red**.
Write **O** on the second flag.
Color the eighth flag **blue**.
Write **D** on the first flag.
Color the sixth flag **yellow**.
Write **G** on the fourth flag.
Color the tenth flag **purple**.
Write **O** on the third flag.
Color the seventh flag **green**.
Color the fifth flag **orange**.
What word did you spell? _____

Swimming in Style!

Directions: Color the swimsuits. The first person is wearing a yellow mask.

Color the fourth suit **brown**.

Color the second suit **purple**.

Color the first suit **red**.

Color the seventh suit pink.

Color the third suit **blue**.

Color the eighth suit **green**.

Color the fifth suit orange.

Color the sixth suit yellow.

Name _____

How Many Robots in All?

Directions: Look at the pictures. Complete the addition sentences.

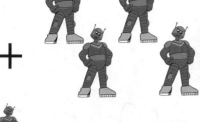

How many 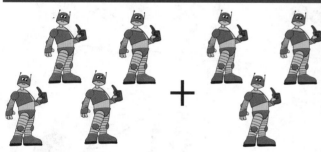s are there in all?

2 + 4 = 6

How many s are there in all?

3 + 5 = ___

How many s are there in all?

4 + 3 = ___

How many s are there in all?

4 + 1 = ___

How many s are there in all?

2 + 5 = ___

How many s are there in all?

4 + 4 = ___

Your Total Solution for Math: Grade 2

How Many Rabbits?

Directions: Look at the pictures. Complete the addition sentences.

How many 🐰s are there in all?

$1 + 1 = \underline{2}$

How many 🐰s are there in all?

$3 + 6 = \underline{}$

How many 🐰s are there in all?

$6 + 1 = \underline{}$

How many 🐰s are there in all?

$3 + 4 = \underline{}$

How many 🐰s are there in all?

$4 + 5 = \underline{}$

How many 🐰s are there in all?

$2 + 3 = \underline{}$

Name _____

Signs of Gain

Directions: Roll a die. Write the addend from the die in the top box. Add to find the sum. Roll again to make each sentence different.

Your Total Solution for Math: Grade 2

How Many in All?

Directions: Count the number in each group and write the number on the line. Then, add the groups together and write the sum.

 _____ strawberries

 _____ strawberries

How many in all? _____

 _____ cookies

 _____ cookies

How many in all? _____

 _____ shoes

 _____ shoes

How many in all? _____

 _____ balloons

 _____ balloons

How many in all? _____

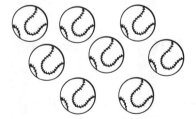 _____ balls

   _____ balls

How many in all? _____

 _____ flowers

 _____ flowers

How many in all? _____

Name _____

Adding 1

Directions: Write a number in the top box of each problem. Complete the problem. Make each problem different.

Your Total Solution for Math: Grade 2

Counting Up

Directions: Count up to get the sum. Write the missing addend in each blank.

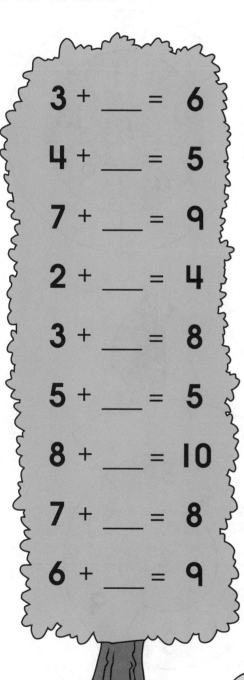

3 + ___ = 6

4 + ___ = 5

7 + ___ = 9

2 + ___ = 4

3 + ___ = 8

5 + ___ = 5

8 + ___ = 10

7 + ___ = 8

6 + ___ = 9

8 + ___ = 9

4 + ___ = 6

6 + ___ = 6

5 + ___ = 7

4 + ___ = 7

9 + ___ = 10

5 + ___ = 8

7 + ___ = 10

6 + ___ = 8

Name _____

Target Practice

Directions: Add the numbers from the inside out. The first one has been done for you.

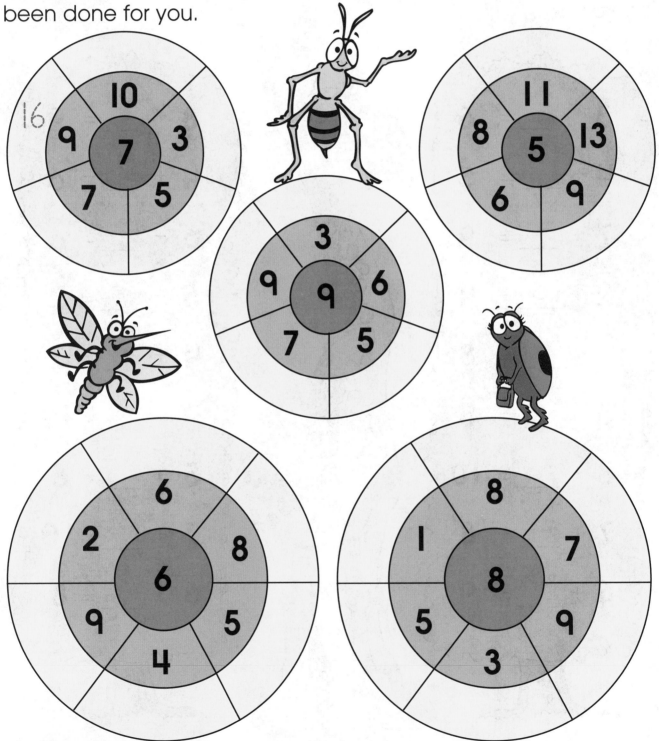

Name _____

It's All the Same

Directions: Count the objects and fill in the blanks. Then, switch the addends and write another addition sentence.

Example:

If ___**3**___ + ___**8**___ = ___**II**___ , so does ___**8**___ + ___**3**___ .

If _____ + _____ = _____ , so does _____ + _____ .

If _____ + _____ = _____ , so does _____ + _____ .

If _____ + _____ = _____ , so does _____ + _____ .

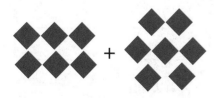

If _____ + _____ = _____ , so does _____ + _____ .

Name _____

Ride the Rapids

Directions: Write each problem on the life jacket with the correct answer.

8 + 5	8 + 6	7 + 5	8 + 4	4 + 9
6 + 6	9 + 7	9 + 5	6 + 7	5 + 9
7 + 8	7 + 9	8 + 9	8 + 8	
6 + 9	7 + 6	5 + 8	3 + 9	
9 + 3	5 + 7	8 + 7	7 + 7	
6 + 8	9 + 8	9 + 6	9 + 4	

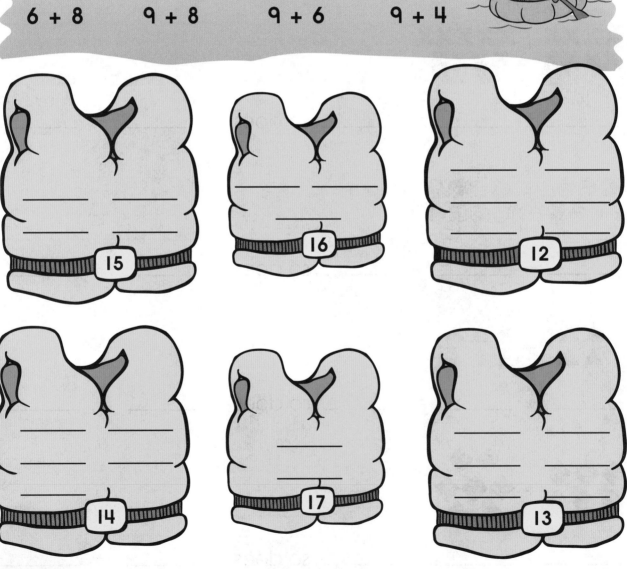

15   16   12

14   17   13

Your Total Solution for Math: Grade 2

Math-Minded Mermaids

Directions: Look at each number. Then, look in each seashell. Circle each pair of numbers that can be added together to equal that number.

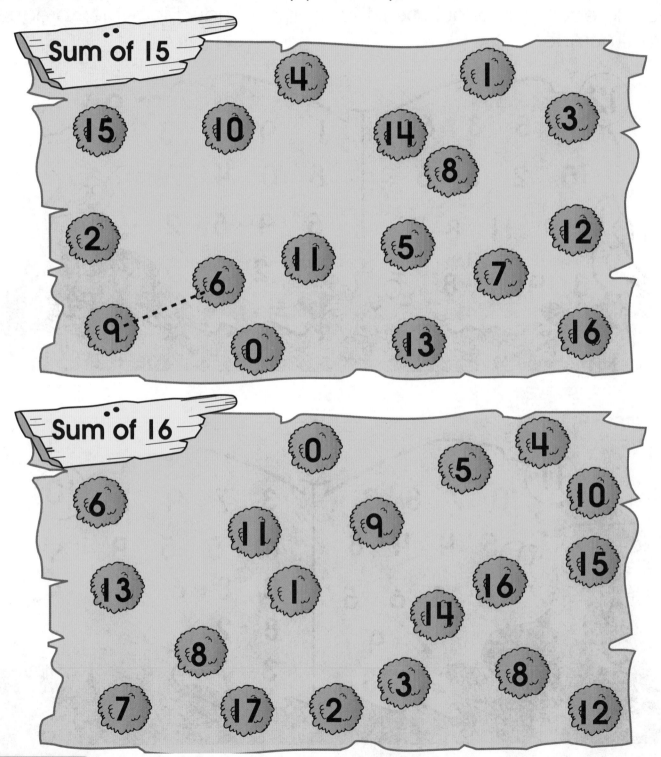
Name _____

Lots of Number Partners

Directions: Connect as many pairs as you can to make each sum.

Sum of 15

4 1
15 10 14 3
8
2 12
5
11 6 7
9 13 16
0

Sum of 16

0 4
5
6 10
11 9
15
13 1 16
14
8 8
3
7 17 2 12

Your Total Solution for Math: Grade 2

Snorkeling Solutions

Directions: Add the numbers in each mask. Write the sums in the bubbles. Color the bubbles of the four largest sums.

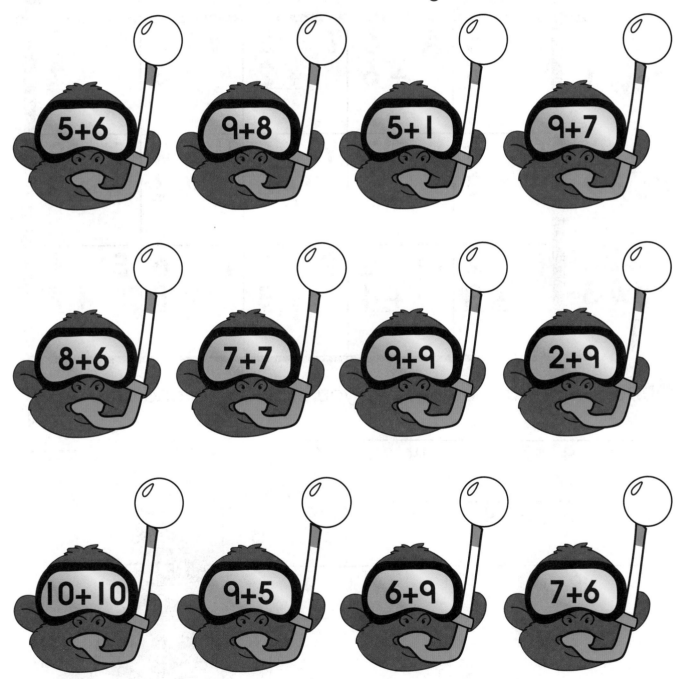

Name _____

Solve the Riddle

Directions: Add to find the sums. Connect the dots in order. Use the sums and letters from the boxes to answer the riddle.

Row 1	G 5 +3	A 6 +6	T 2 +2	W 7 +6	C 3 +2
Row 2	L 8 +8	R 7 +8	Y 5 +5	U 4 +3	E 9 +9
Row 3	N 2 +9	O 5 +4	P 9 +8	I 6 +8	E 1 +2

RIDDLE: What will you get when you cross an eel and a goat?

___ ___ ___ ___ ___ ___ ___
10 9   7   13 14 16 16

___ ___ ___ ___ ___
8   18 4   12 11

___ ___ ___ ___ ___ ___ ___ ___
3   16 18 5   4   15 14 5

___ ___ ___
5   12 11

___ ___ ___ ___ ___ ___
9   17 18 11 18 15

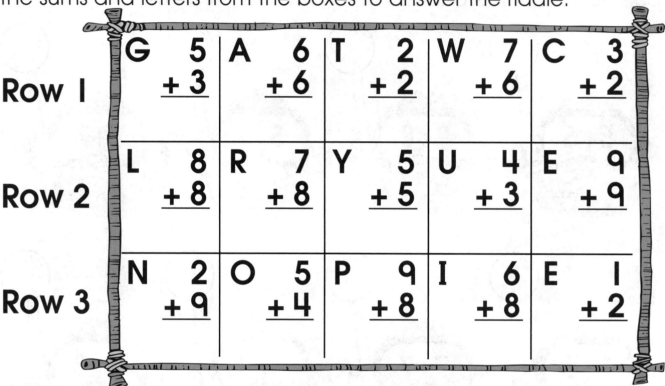

Your Total Solution for Math: Grade 2

Coloring by Number

Directions: Find each sum.
If the sum is **13**, color the space **brown**.
If the sum is **14**, color the space yellow.
If the sum is **16**, color the space **red**.
If the sum is **17**, color the space **blue**.

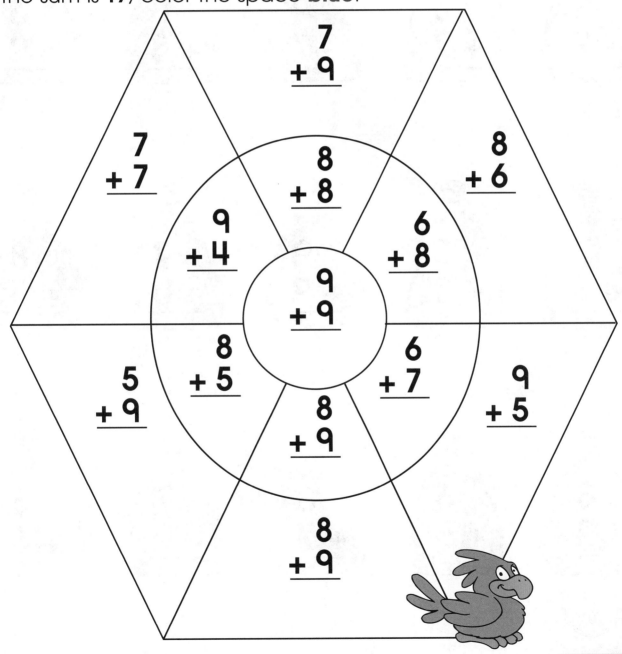

Name _____

Counting Up the Coins

Directions: Solve the problem on each bag. Write the answer on the coin below it. Color the odd sums yellow.

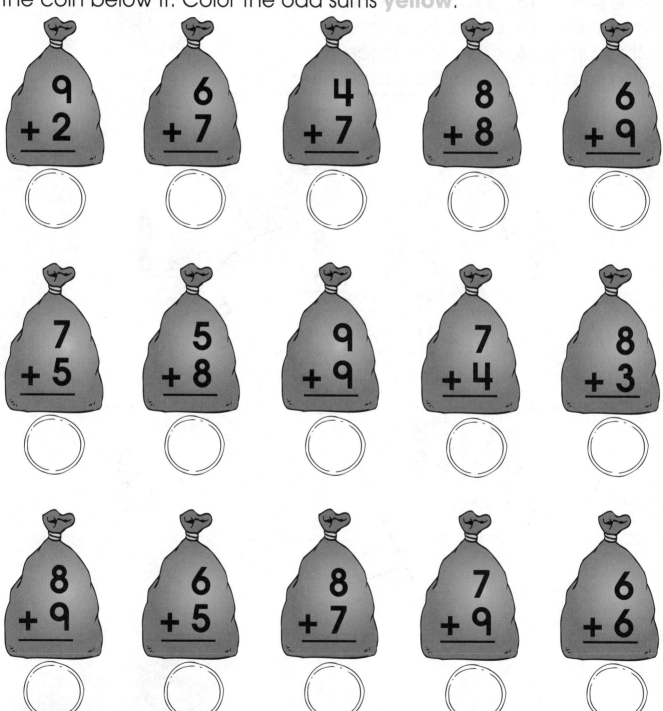

Your Total Solution for Math: Grade 2

Mys-sss-terious Music

Directions: Solve the problems. Color the spaces using the answers.

ANSWER COLOR KEY:

■ = 0 – 2
■ = 3 – 6
■ = 7 – 9
■ = 10 – 12
■ = 13 – 16
■ = 17 – 20

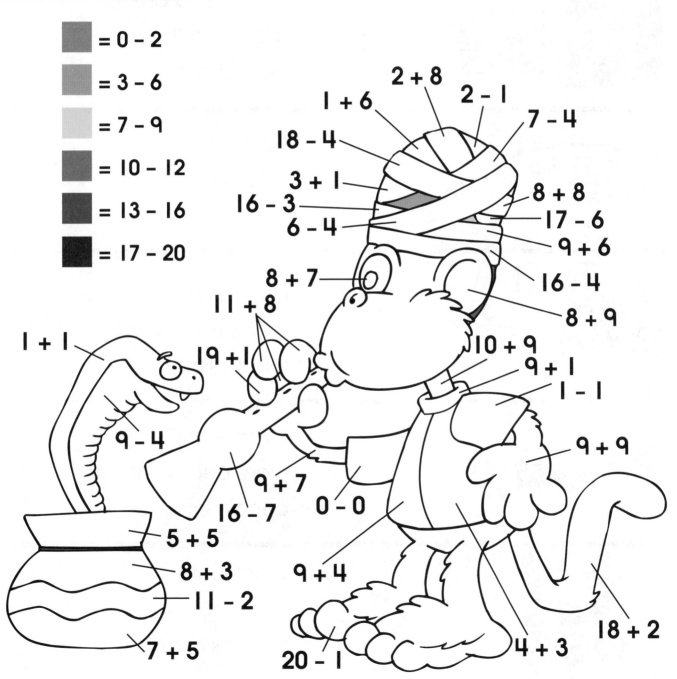

Name _____

Problem Solving

Directions: Solve each problem.

  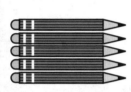

6
+ 5
_____

pencils in a box

more pencils

pencils in all

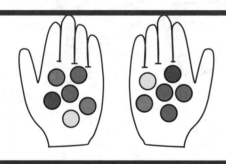

grapes on a plate

more grapes

grapes in all

marbles in one hand

marbles in the other hand

marbles in all

people at the table

more people coming in

people in all

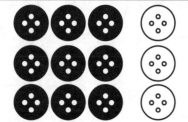

black buttons

white buttons

buttons in all

Your Total Solution for Math: Grade 2

Problem Solving

Directions: Solve each problem.
Example:

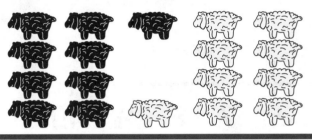

black sheep

white sheep

sheep in all

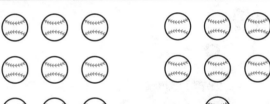

softballs

baseballs

balls in all

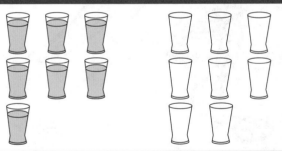

glasses of milkshakes

empty glasses

glasses in all

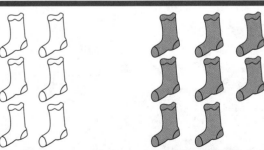

white socks

gray socks

socks in all

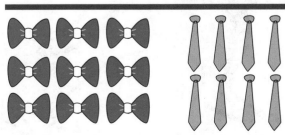

bow ties

regular ties

ties in all

Name _____

Hop Along Numbers

Directions: Use the number line to count back.

Example: 8, _7_ , _6_

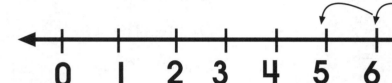

 7 – 3 = ___

7,___,___,___

 6 – 2 = ___

6,___,___

 8 – 1 = ___

8,___

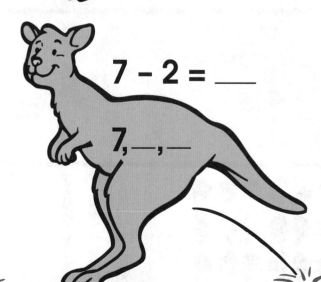 7 – 2 = ___

7,___,___

Your Total Solution for Math: Grade 2

Name _____

Bubbly Baths

Directions: Solve the subtraction sentences below. Write each answer on a rubber duck.

Name _____

Leaves Leaving the Limb

Directions: Subtract to find the difference. Use the code to color the leaves. Code: **0 = green   I = red   2 = yellow   3 = brown**

Row 1:
- $1 - 0$
- $5 - 2$
- $3 - 3$
- $2 - 1$

Row 2:
- $3 - 1$
- $2 - 2$
- $4 - 2$
- $5 - 3$

Row 3:
- $3 - 0$
- $5 - 4$
- $1 - 1$
- $2 - 1$

How many of each color?

 _____   _____   _____   _____

Your Total Solution for Math: Grade 2

Name _____

Differences in Boxes

Directions: Color the two numbers in each box that show the given difference.

Difference of 1

6	4		3	1		4	0
3	8		5	6		1	7

Difference of 1

3	7		2	3		6	3
1	8		5	7		9	7

Difference of 2

3	0		3	8		7	1
7	1		6	9		4	6

Difference of 2

3	4		7	4		10	8
8	2		10	5		5	4

Difference of 0

2	1		7	3		5	6
4	2		8	3		5	4

Name _____

Subtraction Makes Al Tired

Directions: Write a different problem for each answer.

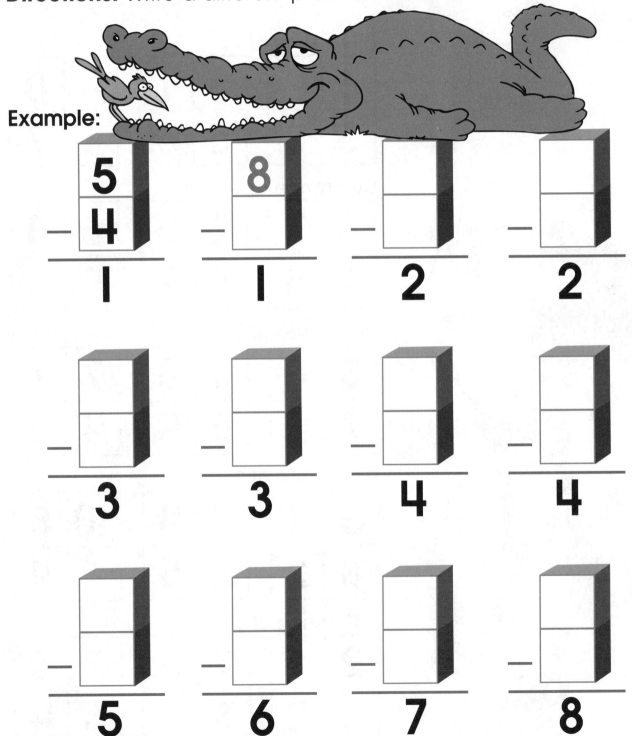

Example:

Your Total Solution for Math: Grade 2

Looping Differences

Directions: Circle the two numbers next to each other that make the given difference. Find as many as you can in each row.

Difference of 1

2	3	0	(8	7)	2	9	10	6	5	1	4	4	3

Difference of 1

8	4	5	3	7	1	2	4	9	8	0	1	7	6

Difference of 2

5	4	2	3	1	0	3	5	8	9	3	6	8	5

Difference of 2

7	5	10	8	1	4	6	3	2	6	7	9	2	0

Difference of 3

1	6	3	2	8	4	7	6	10	0	3	9	5	2

Name _____

Hidden Differences of 2

Directions: Circle the pairs that have a difference of **2**.

Your Total Solution for Math: Grade 2

Hidden Differences of 3

Directions: Circle the pairs that have a difference of **3**.

Name _____

Gone Fishing

Directions: Complete the subtraction sentences to make each problem correct.

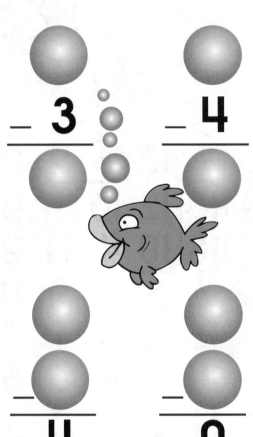

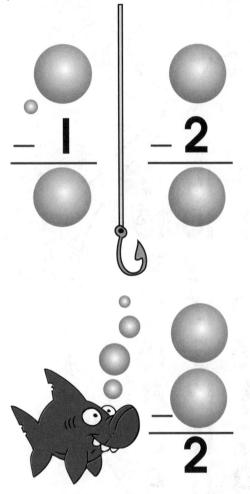

$$\begin{array}{r} \bigcirc \\ -\ 1 \\ \hline \bigcirc \end{array} \qquad \begin{array}{r} \bigcirc \\ -\ 2 \\ \hline \bigcirc \end{array} \qquad \begin{array}{r} \bigcirc \\ -\ 3 \\ \hline \bigcirc \end{array} \qquad \begin{array}{r} \bigcirc \\ -\ 4 \\ \hline \bigcirc \end{array} \qquad \begin{array}{r} \bigcirc \\ -\ 5 \\ \hline \bigcirc \end{array}$$

$$\begin{array}{r} \bigcirc \\ \bigcirc \\ \hline 2 \end{array} \qquad \begin{array}{r} \bigcirc \\ \bigcirc \\ \hline 4 \end{array} \qquad \begin{array}{r} \bigcirc \\ \bigcirc \\ \hline 0 \end{array} \qquad \begin{array}{r} \bigcirc \\ \bigcirc \\ \hline 3 \end{array}$$

$$\begin{array}{r} 5 \\ \bigcirc \\ -\ \bigcirc \\ \hline \bigcirc \end{array} \qquad \begin{array}{r} 6 \\ \bigcirc \\ -\ \bigcirc \\ \hline \bigcirc \end{array} \qquad \begin{array}{r} 7 \\ \bigcirc \\ -\ \bigcirc \\ \hline \bigcirc \end{array} \qquad \begin{array}{r} 8 \\ \bigcirc \\ -\ \bigcirc \\ \hline \bigcirc \end{array} \qquad \begin{array}{r} 9 \\ \bigcirc \\ -\ \bigcirc \\ \hline \bigcirc \end{array}$$

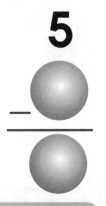

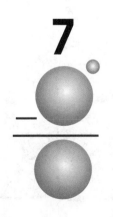

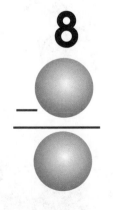

Your Total Solution for Math: Grade 2

Name _____

A Nose for Subtraction

Directions: Cut out the elephant heads at the bottom of the page. Glue each head on the body with the correct answer.

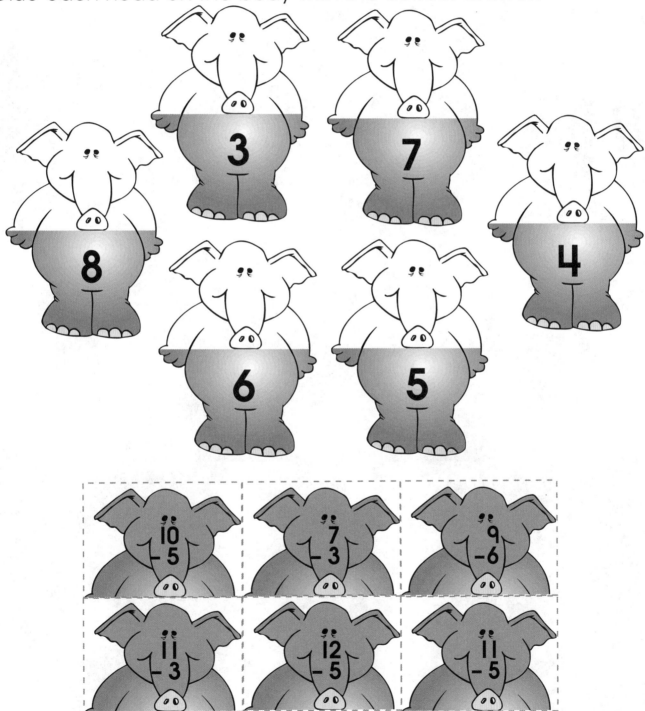

© Carson-Dellosa • CD-704555

Crayon Count

Directions: Count the crayons. Write the number on the blank. Circle the problems that equal the answer.

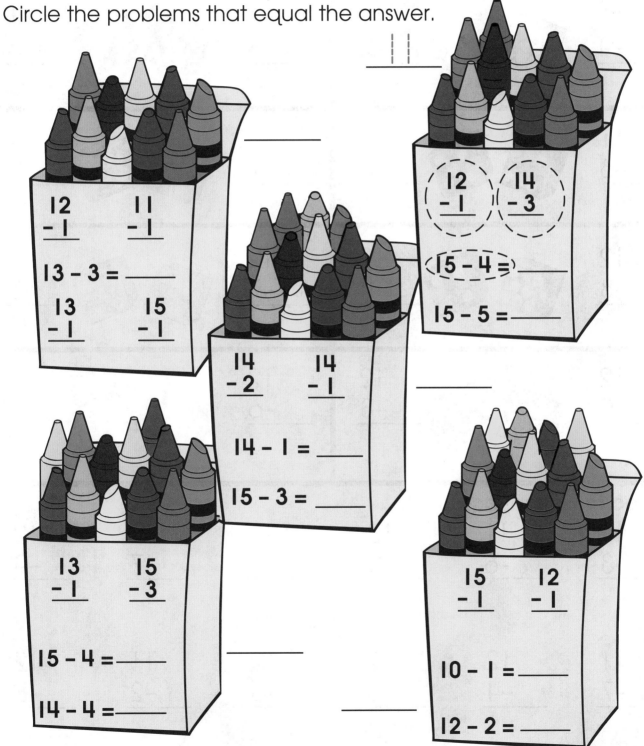

12	11
− 1	− 1

13 − 3 = _____

13	15
− 1	− 1

_____ 11

12	14
− 1	− 3

15 − 4 = _____

15 − 5 = _____

14	14
− 2	− 1

14 − 1 = _____

15 − 3 = _____

13	15
− 1	− 3

15 − 4 = _____

14 − 4 = _____

15	12
− 1	− 1

10 − 1 = _____

12 − 2 = _____

Name _____

Subtraction Facts Through 12

Directions: Subtract.

11
−9
_____

11
−2
_____

11
−8
_____

11
−3
_____

11
−6
_____

11
−5
_____

11
−7
_____

11
−4
_____

12
−8
_____

12
−4
_____

12
−7
_____

12
−5
_____

12
−9
_____

12
−3
_____

12
−6
_____
   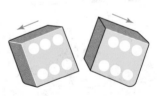

Directions: Subtract.

11 −3	11 −6	12 −3	11 −8	12 −7	12 −9

11 −7	12 −4	12 −5	12 −6	11 −2	12 −8

Your Total Solution for Math: Grade 2

Subtraction Facts Through 18

Directions: Subtract.

Example:

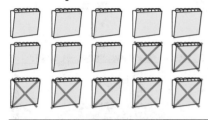

$$
\begin{array}{r} 15 \\ -\ 7 \\ \hline 8 \end{array}
$$

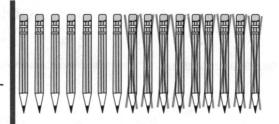

$$
\begin{array}{r} 16 \\ -\ 9 \\ \hline \end{array}
$$

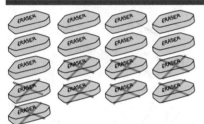

$$
\begin{array}{r} 17 \\ -\ 8 \\ \hline \end{array}
$$

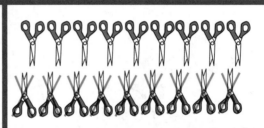

$$
\begin{array}{r} 18 \\ -\ 9 \\ \hline \end{array}
$$

Directions: Subtract.

$\begin{array}{r} 18 \\ -\ 9 \\ \hline \end{array}$	$\begin{array}{r} 13 \\ -\ 5 \\ \hline \end{array}$	$\begin{array}{r} 16 \\ -\ 8 \\ \hline \end{array}$	$\begin{array}{r} 17 \\ -\ 9 \\ \hline \end{array}$	$\begin{array}{r} 14 \\ -\ 6 \\ \hline \end{array}$	$\begin{array}{r} 13 \\ -\ 9 \\ \hline \end{array}$
$\begin{array}{r} 17 \\ -\ 8 \\ \hline \end{array}$	$\begin{array}{r} 15 \\ -\ 9 \\ \hline \end{array}$	$\begin{array}{r} 14 \\ -\ 5 \\ \hline \end{array}$	$\begin{array}{r} 13 \\ -\ 6 \\ \hline \end{array}$	$\begin{array}{r} 16 \\ -\ 7 \\ \hline \end{array}$	$\begin{array}{r} 12 \\ -\ 4 \\ \hline \end{array}$
$\begin{array}{r} 14 \\ -\ 7 \\ \hline \end{array}$	$\begin{array}{r} 15 \\ -\ 8 \\ \hline \end{array}$	$\begin{array}{r} 16 \\ -\ 9 \\ \hline \end{array}$	$\begin{array}{r} 12 \\ -\ 7 \\ \hline \end{array}$	$\begin{array}{r} 15 \\ -\ 7 \\ \hline \end{array}$	$\begin{array}{r} 13 \\ -\ 4 \\ \hline \end{array}$
$\begin{array}{r} 15 \\ -\ 6 \\ \hline \end{array}$	$\begin{array}{r} 14 \\ -\ 8 \\ \hline \end{array}$	$\begin{array}{r} 12 \\ -\ 3 \\ \hline \end{array}$	$\begin{array}{r} 13 \\ -\ 9 \\ \hline \end{array}$	$\begin{array}{r} 14 \\ -\ 9 \\ \hline \end{array}$	$\begin{array}{r} 11 \\ -\ 3 \\ \hline \end{array}$

Name _____

"Grrreat" Picture

Directions: Subtract. Write the answer in the space. Then, color the spaces according to the answers.

1 = white	2 = purple	3 = black	4 = green	5 = yellow
6 = blue	7 = pink	8 = gray	9 = orange	10 = red

   Your Total Solution for Math: Grade 2

Connect the Facts

Directions: Solve the subtraction problems below.

Name _____

Swamp Stories

Directions: Read the story. Subtract to find the difference. Write the number in the box.

$$\begin{array}{r} 4 \\ -\ 1 \\ \hline \ \end{array}$$

4 alligators were in the water. 1 got out. How many alligators were left in the water?

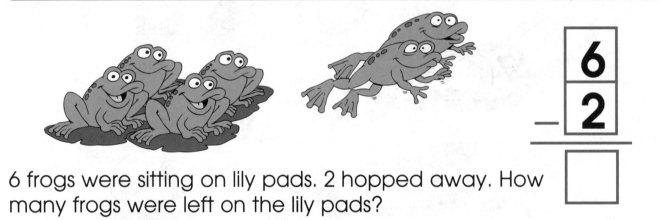

$$\begin{array}{r} 6 \\ -\ 2 \\ \hline \ \end{array}$$

6 frogs were sitting on lily pads. 2 hopped away. How many frogs were left on the lily pads?

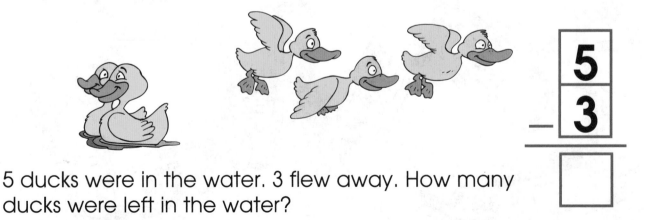

$$\begin{array}{r} 5 \\ -\ 3 \\ \hline \ \end{array}$$

5 ducks were in the water. 3 flew away. How many ducks were left in the water?

Your Total Solution for Math: Grade 2

More Animal Stories

Directions: Subtract to find the difference. Cut out the subtraction sentences and glue them in the correct boxes. Write the difference in each small box.

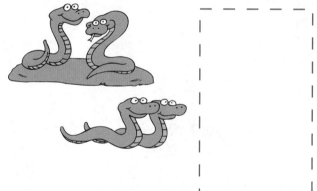

How many toucans were left?   How many lion cubs were left?

How many monkeys were left?   How many snakes were left?

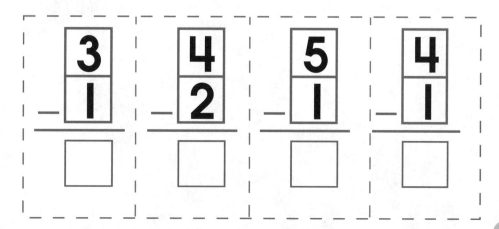

$$-\frac{\begin{array}{r}3\\1\end{array}}{} \qquad -\frac{\begin{array}{r}4\\2\end{array}}{} \qquad -\frac{\begin{array}{r}5\\1\end{array}}{} \qquad -\frac{\begin{array}{r}4\\1\end{array}}{}$$

Facts Through 5

Directions: Add or subtract.

Examples:

```
  1         2         2         1         3         3
+ 1       - 1       + 1       + 2       - 1       - 2
---       ---       ---       ---       ---       ---
  2         1
```

```
  3         1              2                   4         0
+ 1       + 3           + 2                  + 0       + 4
---       ---           ---                  ---       ---


  4         4              4                   4         4
- 1       - 3           - 2                  - 0       - 4
---       ---           ---                  ---       ---
```

```
  3         2              4         1              5         0
+ 2       + 3           + 1       + 4           + 0       + 5
---       ---           ---       ---           ---       ---


  5         5              5         5              5         5
- 2       - 3           - 1       - 4           - 0       - 5
---       ---           ---       ---           ---       ---
```

Name _____

Facts for 6 and 7

Directions: Add or subtract.

Examples:

$$\begin{array}{r} 5 \\ +\ 1 \\ \hline 6 \end{array} \qquad \begin{array}{r} 1 \\ +\ 5 \\ \hline \end{array} \qquad \begin{array}{r} 6 \\ -\ 1 \\ \hline 5 \end{array} \qquad \begin{array}{r} 6 \\ -\ 5 \\ \hline \end{array}$$

$$\begin{array}{r} 3 \\ +\ 3 \\ \hline \end{array} \qquad \begin{array}{r} 6 \\ -\ 3 \\ \hline \end{array} \qquad\qquad \begin{array}{r} 4 \\ +\ 2 \\ \hline \end{array} \qquad \begin{array}{r} 2 \\ +\ 4 \\ \hline \end{array} \qquad \begin{array}{r} 6 \\ -\ 2 \\ \hline \end{array} \qquad \begin{array}{r} 6 \\ -\ 4 \\ \hline \end{array}$$

$$\begin{array}{r} 4 \\ +\ 3 \\ \hline \end{array} \qquad \begin{array}{r} 3 \\ +\ 4 \\ \hline \end{array} \qquad \begin{array}{r} 5 \\ +\ 2 \\ \hline \end{array} \qquad \begin{array}{r} 2 \\ +\ 5 \\ \hline \end{array} \qquad \begin{array}{r} 6 \\ +\ 1 \\ \hline \end{array} \qquad \begin{array}{r} 1 \\ +\ 6 \\ \hline \end{array}$$

$$\begin{array}{r} 7 \\ -\ 3 \\ \hline \end{array} \qquad \begin{array}{r} 7 \\ -\ 4 \\ \hline \end{array} \qquad \begin{array}{r} 7 \\ -\ 2 \\ \hline \end{array} \qquad \begin{array}{r} 7 \\ -\ 5 \\ \hline \end{array} \qquad \begin{array}{r} 7 \\ -\ 1 \\ \hline \end{array} \qquad \begin{array}{r} 7 \\ -\ 6 \\ \hline \end{array}$$

$$\begin{array}{r} 3 \\ +\ 3 \\ \hline \end{array} \qquad \begin{array}{r} 5 \\ +\ 2 \\ \hline \end{array} \qquad \begin{array}{r} 6 \\ +\ 0 \\ \hline \end{array} \qquad \begin{array}{r} 7 \\ -\ 7 \\ \hline \end{array} \qquad \begin{array}{r} 7 \\ -\ 4 \\ \hline \end{array} \qquad \begin{array}{r} 6 \\ -\ 2 \\ \hline \end{array}$$

Facts for 8

Directions: Add or subtract.

Examples:

```
    5          3              8                    8
  + 3        + 5            - 3                  - 5
  -----      -----          -----                -----
    8                         5
```

```
        4                  6          2              7          1
      + 4                + 2        + 6            + 1        + 7
      -----              -----      -----          -----      -----


        8                  8          8              8          8
      - 4                - 2        - 6            - 1        - 7
      -----              -----      -----          -----      -----
```

```
    2          4              5          3              7          0
  + 6        + 3            + 1        + 5            + 1        + 8
  -----      -----          -----      -----          -----      -----


    8          7              8          6              8          8
  - 1        - 6            - 5        - 3            - 0        - 2
  -----      -----          -----      -----          -----      -----
```

Name _____

Facts for 9

Directions: Add or subtract.

Examples:

  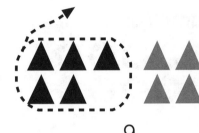

$$\begin{array}{r} 5 \\ + 4 \\ \hline 9 \end{array} \qquad \begin{array}{r} 4 \\ + 5 \\ \hline \end{array} \qquad \begin{array}{r} 9 \\ - 4 \\ \hline 5 \end{array} \qquad \begin{array}{r} 9 \\ - 5 \\ \hline \end{array}$$

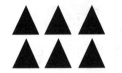 

$$\begin{array}{r} 6 \\ + 3 \\ \hline \end{array} \qquad \begin{array}{r} 3 \\ + 6 \\ \hline \end{array} \qquad \begin{array}{r} 7 \\ + 2 \\ \hline \end{array} \qquad \begin{array}{r} 2 \\ + 7 \\ \hline \end{array} \qquad \begin{array}{r} 8 \\ + 1 \\ \hline \end{array} \qquad \begin{array}{r} 1 \\ + 8 \\ \hline \end{array}$$

$$\begin{array}{r} 9 \\ - 3 \\ \hline \end{array} \qquad \begin{array}{r} 9 \\ - 6 \\ \hline \end{array} \qquad \begin{array}{r} 9 \\ - 2 \\ \hline \end{array} \qquad \begin{array}{r} 9 \\ - 7 \\ \hline \end{array} \qquad \begin{array}{r} 9 \\ - 1 \\ \hline \end{array} \qquad \begin{array}{r} 9 \\ - 8 \\ \hline \end{array}$$

$$\begin{array}{r} 5 \\ + 4 \\ \hline \end{array} \qquad \begin{array}{r} 2 \\ + 7 \\ \hline \end{array} \qquad \begin{array}{r} 6 \\ + 1 \\ \hline \end{array} \qquad \begin{array}{r} 9 \\ + 0 \\ \hline \end{array} \qquad \begin{array}{r} 1 \\ + 8 \\ \hline \end{array} \qquad \begin{array}{r} 4 \\ + 4 \\ \hline \end{array}$$

$$\begin{array}{r} 9 \\ - 5 \\ \hline \end{array} \qquad \begin{array}{r} 7 \\ - 3 \\ \hline \end{array} \qquad \begin{array}{r} 9 \\ - 8 \\ \hline \end{array} \qquad \begin{array}{r} 9 \\ - 3 \\ \hline \end{array} \qquad \begin{array}{r} 9 \\ - 9 \\ \hline \end{array} \qquad \begin{array}{r} 9 \\ - 0 \\ \hline \end{array}$$

Your Total Solution for Math: Grade 2

Facts for 10

Directions: Add or subtract.

Examples:

5 + 5 — 10	6 + 4	4 + 6	7 + 3	3 + 7
10 − 5 — 5	10 − 4	10 − 6	10 − 3	10 − 7

8 + 2	2 + 8	9 + 1	1 + 9
10 − 2	10 − 8	10 − 1	10 − 9

4	5	9	10	10	10
+ 6	+ 5	+ 1	− 8	− 3	− 0

Problem Solving

Directions: Solve each problem.

Example:

$$4$$
$$+\ 3$$
$$\overline{7}$$

leaves on the ground
leaves falling
leaves in all

_____ balls in all
−_____ balls falling
_____ balls not falling

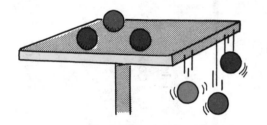

_____ fish by a rock
+_____ more fish coming
_____ fish in all

_____ pencils in all
−_____ pencils taken
_____ pencils not taken

_____ puppies on a rug
+_____ more puppies coming
_____ puppies in all

Your Total Solution for Math: Grade 2

Checkup

Directions: Add.

2 + 4	7 + 3	4 + 5	6 + 2	2 + 3	4 + 0
4 + 3	1 + 5	2 + 8	3 + 3	6 + 4	2 + 1
3 + 1	7 + 0	8 + 1	5 + 2	3 + 6	5 + 5

Directions: Subtract.

3 - 3	5 - 2	10 - 6	9 - 2	7 - 3	10 - 5
9 - 1	8 - 7	1 - 0	6 - 4	8 - 5	10 - 8
9 - 6	4 - 3	6 - 3	7 - 5	10 - 9	8 - 4

Name _____

Addition and Subtraction

Directions: Solve the number problem under each picture. Write **+** or **–** to show if you should add or subtract.

Example:

How many 🏏 s in all?

4 + **5** = ____9____

How many 💧 s in all?

7   **5** = _____

Example:

How many 🪶 s are left?

12 – **3** = ____9____

How many ⭐ s are left?

15   **8** = _____

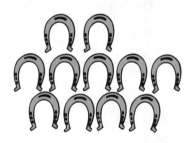

How many 🍬 s in all?

5   **8** = _____

How many ⚲ s are left?

11   **4** = _____

Your Total Solution for Math: Grade 2

Addition and Subtraction

Directions: Solve the number problem under each picture. Write +
or – to show if you should add or subtract.

Example:

How many s in all?

7 + 5 = ___12___

How many s in all?

8 ___ 3 = _____

Example:

How many s are left?

9 – 4 = ___5___

How many 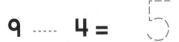s are left?

14 ___ 1 = _____

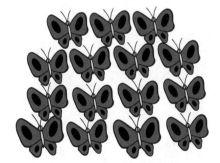

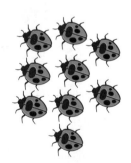

How many s in all?

15 ___ 6 = _____

How many s are left?

9 ___ 5 = _____

Name _____

Hopping Around

Directions: Write the number sentence on the line below each number line.

Example:

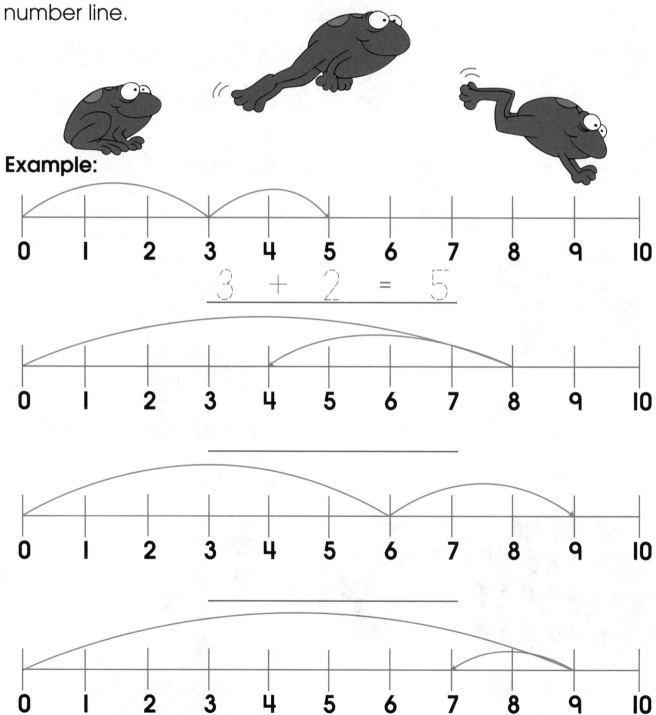

$$3 + 2 = 5$$

Your Total Solution for Math: Grade 2

Sums and Differences

Directions: Color two numbers in each box to show the given sum or difference.

Sum of 8

3	7
1	4

3	6
7	2

6	5
4	4

3	8
1	5

Difference of 1

6	3
1	5

5	9
10	7

8	5
3	2

5	2
4	0

Sum of 9

0	5
6	4

4	3
6	2

8	3
1	2

5	5
7	2

Difference of 2

6	9
1	4

4	10
7	5

5	8
1	10

0	2
7	3

Name _____

Big Families

Directions: Complete each number sentence in each number family.

2	**3**
0 + ___ = 2	1 + 2 = ___
2 + 0 = ___	___ + 1 = 3
___ – 0 = 2	3 – ___ = 2
2 – 2 = ___	3 – 2 = ___

4	**5**
___ + 3 = 4	2 + 3 = ___
3 + 1 = ___	___ + 2 = 5
4 – ___ = 3	5 – ___ = 3
___ – 3 = 1	___ – 3 = 2

6	**6**
2 + ___ = 6	5 + ___ = 6
4 + 2 = ___	___ + ___ = ___
6 – ___ = 4	6 – ___ = 5
6 – 4 = ___	___ – 5 = ___

Your Total Solution for Math: Grade 2

Help the Hippo

Directions: Use the numbers in each thought bubble to write the number family.

Example:

$2 + 1 = 3$
$1 + 2 = 3$
$3 - 1 = 2$
$3 - 2 = 1$

2, 1, 3

2, 4, 6

1, 4, 5

2, 5, 7

3, 4, 7

2, 3, 5

Name _____

Place Value: Ones, Tens

The **place value** of a digit or numeral is shown by where it is in the number. For example, in the number **23**, **2** has the place value of **tens**, and **3** is **ones**.

Directions: Add the tens and ones and write your answers in the blanks.

Example:

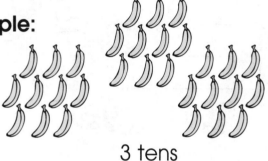

         +   = _33_

3 tens   +   3 ones   = _**33**_

	tens ones		tens ones
7 tens + 5 ones	= _____	4 tens + 0 ones	= _____
2 tens + 3 ones	= _____	8 tens + 1 one	= _____
5 tens + 2 ones	= _____	1 ten + 1 one	= _____
5 tens + 4 ones	= _____	6 tens + 3 ones	= _____
9 tens + 5 ones	= _____		

Directions: Draw a line to the correct number.

6 tens + 7 ones   73
4 tens + 2 ones   67
8 tens + 0 ones   51
7 tens + 3 ones   80
5 tens + 1 one   42

Name _____

Finding Place Value: Ones and Tens

Directions: Write the numbers for the tens and ones. Then add.

Example:

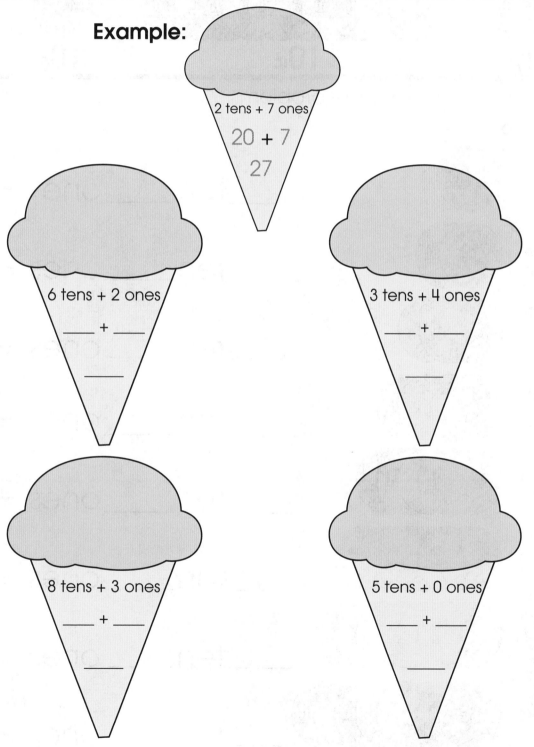

2 tens + 7 ones
20 + 7
27

6 tens + 2 ones
___ + ___
___

3 tens + 4 ones
___ + ___
___

8 tens + 3 ones
___ + ___
___

5 tens + 0 ones
___ + ___
___

Numbers 11 Through 18

1¢   10¢   10¢

Directions: Complete the problems.

Example:

      ___ten ___one = |1

    ___ten ___ones = ___

    ___ten ___ones = ___

    ___ten ___ones = ___

    ___ten ___ones = ___

    ___ten ___ones = ___

    ___ten ___ones = ___

    ___ten ___ones = ___

Numbers 19 Through 39

Directions: Complete the problems.

Example:

__2__ tens   = __20__

_____ tens _____ ones = _____

_____ tens _____ ones = _____

_____ tens _____ ones = _____

_____ tens   = _____

_____ tens _____ ones = _____

_____ tens _____ ones = _____

_____ tens _____ ones = _____

Name _____

Numbers 40 Through 99

Directions: Complete the problems.

Example:

____4____ tens = ___40___

_____ tens _____ ones = _____

_____ tens _____ ones = _____

_____ tens _____ ones = _____

_____ tens = _____

_____ tens _____ ones = _____

_____ tens _____ ones = _____

_____ tens _____ ones = _____

Your Total Solution for Math: Grade 2

Numbers Through 99

Directions: Complete the problems.
Example:

4 tens   6 ones = __46__   2 tens   l one   = _____

l ten   2 ones = _____   5 tens   7 ones = _____

3 tens   7 ones = _____   l ten   9 ones = _____

2 tens   4 ones = _____   8 tens   8 ones = _____

9 tens   = _____   6 tens   7 ones = _____

6 tens   = _____   7 tens   2 ones = _____

5 tens   3 ones = _____   9 tens   5 ones = _____

7 tens   8 ones = _____   4 tens   l one   = _____

l ten   l one = _____   3 tens   4 ones = _____

8 tens   4 ones = _____   6 tens   6 ones = _____

3 tens   5 ones = _____   8 tens   9 ones = _____

4 tens   9 ones = _____   2 tens   = _____

9 tens   6 ones = _____   5 tens   = _____

Name _____

Hundreds, Tens, and Ones

Directions: Count the groups of crayons. Write the number of hundreds, tens, and ones.

Example:

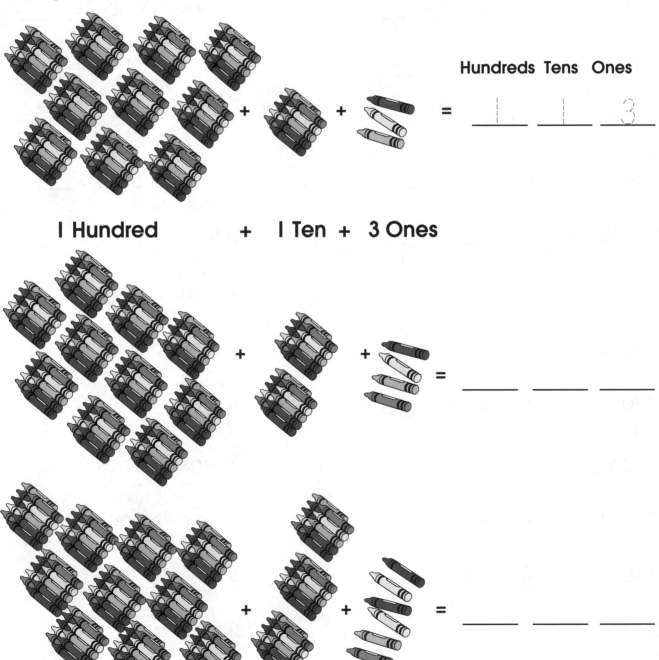

Hundreds Tens Ones

_1_ _1_ _3_

1 Hundred + 1 Ten + 3 Ones

= _____ _____ _____

= _____ _____ _____

Your Total Solution for Math: Grade 2

Name _____

What Big Numbers!

Directions: Write each number.

Example:

Hundreds	Tens	Ones
■	|||	●●

___ hundreds
___ tens
___ ones = __132__

Hundreds	Tens	Ones
■	||||	●●● ●●● ●

___ hundreds
___ tens
___ ones = _____

Hundreds	Tens	Ones
■ ■ ■	|||	●●● ●●● ●●●

___ hundreds
___ tens
___ ones = _____

Hundreds	Tens	Ones
■ ■ ■ ■ ■			●

___ hundreds
___ tens
___ ones = _____

Hundreds	Tens	Ones
■ ■		●●● ●●● ●●●

___ hundreds
___ tens
___ ones = _____

Hundreds	Tens	Ones
■ ■ ■ ■ ■ ■					
	●●●

___ hundreds
___ tens
___ ones = _____

Hundreds	Tens	Ones
■ ■ ■	||||	●●● ●●

___ hundreds
___ tens
___ ones = _____

Hundreds	Tens	Ones
■ ■					
			●●● ●●● ●

___ hundreds
___ tens
___ ones = _____

Name _____

Count 'Em Up!

Directions: Look at the example. Then, write the missing numbers in the blanks.

Example:

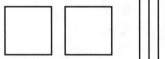

2 hundreds + 3 tens + 6 ones =

hundreds	tens	ones	
2	3	6	= 236

	hundreds	tens	ones	
3 hundreds + 4 tens + 8 ones =	3	4	8	= _____
__ hundreds + __ ten + __ ones =	2	1	7	= _____
__ hundreds + __ tens + __ ones =	6	3	5	= _____
__ hundreds + __ tens + __ ones =	4	7	9	= _____
__ hundreds + __ tens + __ ones =	2	9	4	= _____
__ hundreds + __ tens + __ ones =	4	2	0	= _____
3 hundreds + 1 ten + 3 ones = ____	____	____	= _____
3 hundreds + __ tens + 7 ones = ____		5	____	= _____
6 hundreds + 2 tens + __ ones = ____			8	= _____

© Carson-Dellosa • CD-704555

Your Total Solution for Math: Grade 2

Name _____

Up, Up, and Away

Directions: Use the code to color the balloons. If the answer has:

7 hundreds, color it **red**.
6 hundreds, color it **green**.
5 hundreds, color it **orange**.
8 tens, color it **yellow**.
3 ones, color it **brown**.

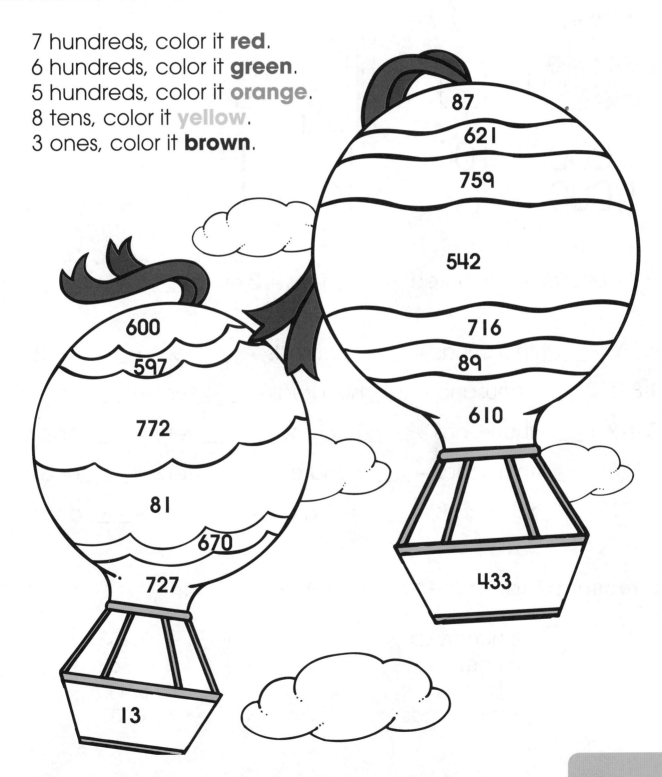

Name _____

Place Value: Thousands

Directions: Study the example. Write the missing numbers.
Example:

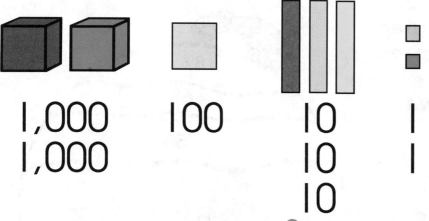

1,000	100	10	1
1,000		10	1
		10	

2 thousands + 1 hundred + __3__ tens + 2 ones = __2,132__

5,286 = ____ thousands + ____ hundreds + ____ tens + ____ ones

1,831 = ____ thousand + ____ hundreds + ____ tens + ____ one

8,972 = ____ thousands + ____ hundreds + ____ tens + ____ ones

4,528 = ____ thousands + ____ hundreds + ____ tens + ____ ones

3,177 = ____ thousands + ____ hundred + ____ tens + ____ ones

Directions: Draw a line to the number that has:

8 hundreds	7,103
5 ones	2,862
9 tens	5,996
7 thousands	1,485

Your Total Solution for Math: Grade 2

Place Value: Thousands

6, 4 3 1
thousands | hundreds | tens | ones

Directions: Tell which number is in each place.

 Thousands place:

2,456   4,621   3,456

_____   _____   _____

 Tens place:

4,286   1,234   5,678

_____   _____   _____

 Hundreds place:

6,321   3,210   7,871

_____   _____   _____

⭐ Ones place:

5,432   6,531   9,980

_____   _____   _____

Name _____

Two-Digit Addition

Directions: Study the example. Follow the steps to add.

Example:
$$33$$
$$+41$$

Step 1: Add the ones.

tens	ones
3	3
+4	1
	4

Step 2: Add the tens.

tens	ones
3	3
+4	1
7	4

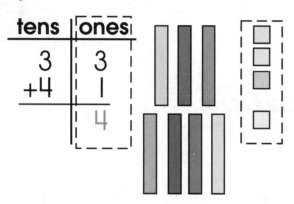

tens	ones
4	2
+2	4
6	6

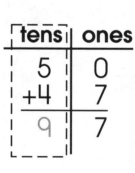

tens	ones
5	0
+4	7
9	7

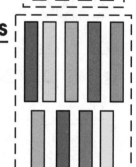

24	15	38	11	37	72	33	10
+62	+23	+61	+26	+42	+11	+51	+30

25	62	32	25	82	91	16	55
+42	+14	+44	+13	+ 6	+ 5	+71	+ 3

     Your Total Solution for Math: Grade 2

Two-Digit Addition

Directions: Add the total points scored in each game. Remember to add **ones** first and **tens** second.

Example:

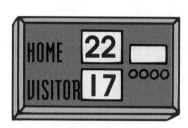

Total __39__

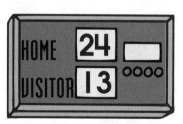

Total _____

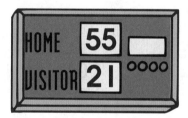

Total _____

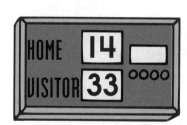

Total _____

Total _____

Total _____

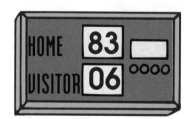

Total _____

Total _____

Total _____

Adding Tens

3 tens	30	6 tens	60
+ 4 tens	+40	+ 2 tens	+20
7 tens	70	8 tens	80

Directions: Add.

2 tens	20		6 tens	60
+ 4 tens	+40		+ 2 tens	+20
tens			tens	

20	10	40	30	50
+20	+50	+20	+40	+30

30	60	20	70	10
+20	+10	+50	+10	+10

10	40	80	60	20
+20	+40	+10	+30	+60

70	40	30	50	30
+20	+10	+10	+40	+30

Your Total Solution for Math: Grade 2

Problem Solving

Directions: Solve each problem.
Example:

There are 20 men in the plane.
30 women get in the plane.

How many men and women are in the plane?

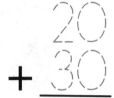

Jill buys 10 apples.
Carol buys 20 apples.

How many apples in all?

There are 30 ears of corn in one pile.
There are 50 ears of corn in another pile.

How many ears of corn in all?

Henry cut 40 pieces of wood.
Art cut 20 pieces of wood.

How many pieces of wood were cut?

Adolpho had 60 baseball cards.
Maria had 30 baseball cards.

How many baseball cards in all?

   Name _____

Digital Addition

Add the ones.

tens	ones
2	4
+ 3	2
	6

Then, add the tens.

tens	ones
2	4
+ 3	2
5	6

Directions: Solve the addition problems below.

tens	ones
1	7
+ 2	1

tens	ones
3	4
+ 5	2

tens	ones
	5
+ 6	2

tens	ones
	6
+ 5	2

tens	ones
2	0
+ 4	0

tens	ones
5	1
+	8

tens	ones
7	2
+ 1	7

tens	ones
4	7
+ 2	1

tens	ones
2	5
+ 6	2

tens	ones
4	2
+ 2	4

tens	ones
8	3
+ 1	4

tens	ones
3	2
+ 2	5

     Your Total Solution for Math: Grade 2

Circus Fun

Directions: Add to solve the problems. Add the ones first. Then, add the tens.

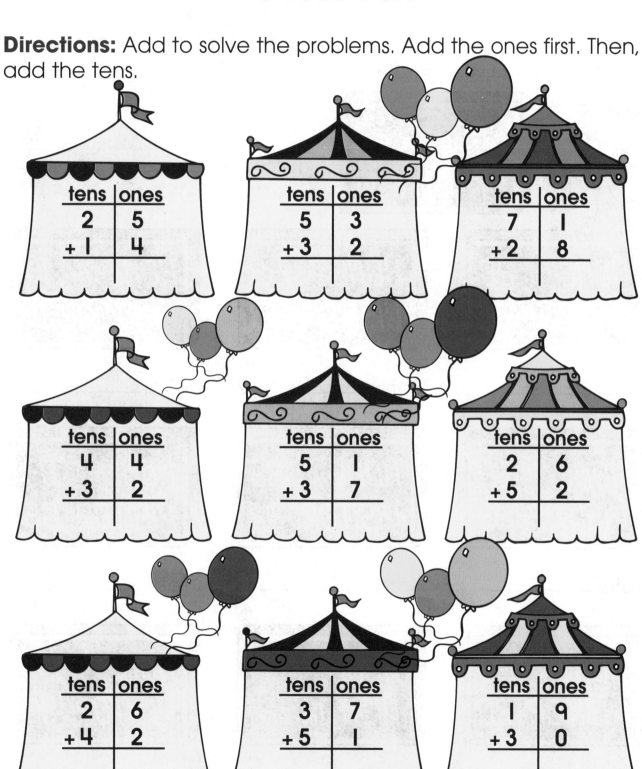

tens	ones
2	5
+1	4

tens	ones
5	3
+3	2

tens	ones
7	1
+2	8

tens	ones
4	4
+3	2

tens	ones
5	1
+3	7

tens	ones
2	6
+5	2

tens	ones
2	6
+4	2

tens	ones
3	7
+5	1

tens	ones
1	9
+3	0

Scoreboard Sums

Directions: Add the total points scored in each game. Remember to add the ones first, then the tens.

Example:

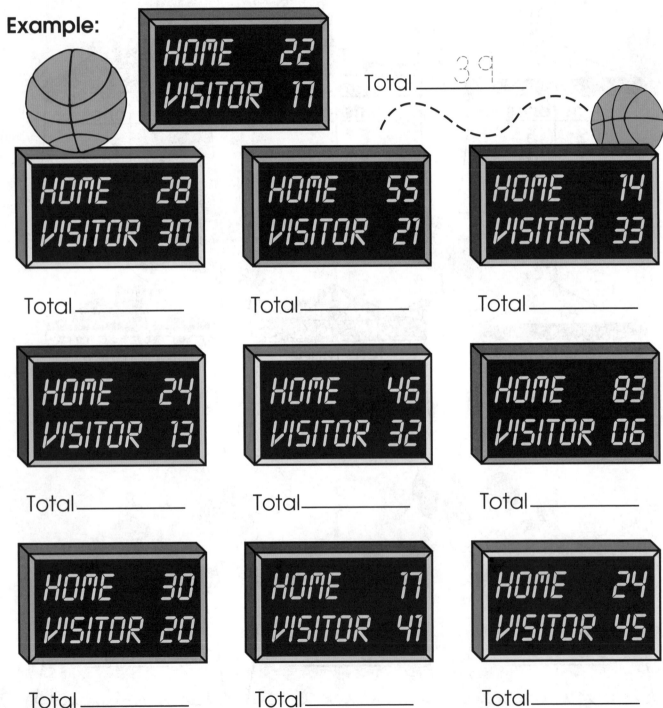

HOME 22
VISITOR 17

Total _____39_____

HOME 28
VISITOR 30

Total _____

HOME 55
VISITOR 21

Total _____

HOME 14
VISITOR 33

Total _____

HOME 24
VISITOR 13

Total _____

HOME 46
VISITOR 32

Total _____

HOME 83
VISITOR 06

Total _____

HOME 30
VISITOR 20

Total _____

HOME 17
VISITOR 41

Total _____

HOME 24
VISITOR 45

Total _____

     Your Total Solution for Math: Grade 2

Anchors Away

Directions: Solve the addition problems. Use the code to find the answer to this riddle:

What did the pirate have to do before every trip out to sea?

48	36	58	96	69	75	89	29
O	H	G	B	T	E	N	A

Example:

42 +16	34 +41	60 + 9
58		

G		

17 +31	55 +34

26 +43	14 +22	52 +23

83 +13	24 +24	5 +24	52 +17

			!

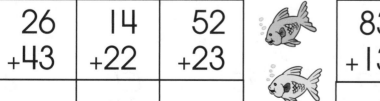

Name _____

Two-Digit Subtraction

Directions: Look at the example.
Follow the steps to subtract.

Examples:

$$\begin{array}{r} 24 \\ -14 \\ \hline \end{array} \qquad \begin{array}{r} 24 \\ -12 \\ \hline \end{array}$$

Step 1: Subtract the ones.

tens	ones
2	8
-1	4
	4

Step 2: Subtract the tens.

tens	ones
2	8
-1	4
1	4

Step 1: Subtract the ones.

tens	ones
2	4
-1	2
	2

Step 2: Subtract the tens.

tens	ones
2	4
-1	2
1	2

$$\begin{array}{r} 24 \\ -12 \\ \hline \end{array} \qquad \begin{array}{r} 61 \\ -30 \\ \hline \end{array} \qquad \begin{array}{r} 77 \\ -44 \\ \hline \end{array} \qquad \begin{array}{r} 85 \\ -24 \\ \hline \end{array} \qquad \begin{array}{r} 57 \\ -23 \\ \hline \end{array} \qquad \begin{array}{r} 87 \\ -33 \\ \hline \end{array}$$

Your Total Solution for Math: Grade 2

Subtracting Tens

Examples:

6 tens	6 0		8 tens	8 0
− 3 tens	− 3 0		− 2 tens	− 2 0
3 tens	3 0		6 tens	60

Directions: Subtract.

7 tens	7 0		4 tens	4 0
− 5 tens	− 5 0		− 2 tens	− 2 0
tens			tens	

5 0	6 0	2 0	8 0	4 0
− 3 0	− 2 0	− 1 0	− 4 0	− 4 0

9 0	8 0	7 0	3 0	5 0
− 5 0	− 2 0	− 3 0	− 2 0	− 4 0

6 0	4 0	8 0	9 0	7 0
− 3 0	− 1 0	− 3 0	− 2 0	− 5 0

8 0	9 0	7 0	6 0	5 0
− 7 0	− 8 0	− 4 0	− 4 0	− 2 0

Name _____

Problem Solving

Directions: Solve each problem.

Example:

Mr. Cobb counts 70 ✏️ s.

He sells 30 ✏️ s.

How many ✏️ s are left?

$$\begin{array}{r} 70 \\ -\,30 \\ \hline 40 \end{array}$$

Keith has 20 🔨 s.

Leon has 10 🔨 s.

How many more 🔨 s does Keith have than Leon?

Tina plants 60 🌸 s.

Melody plants 30 🌸 s.

How many more 🌸 s did Tina plant than Melody?

Link has 80 ⚫ s.

Jessica has 50 ⚫ s .

How many more ⚫ s does Link have than Jessica?

Maranda hits 40 ⚾ s.

Harold hits 30 ⚾ s.

How many more ⚾ s does Maranda hit than Harold?

Your Total Solution for Math: Grade 2

Name _____

TWO-DIGIT SUBTRACTION
(NO REGROUPING)

1+2

All Aboard

Directions: Count the tens and ones and write the numbers. Then, subtract to solve the problems.

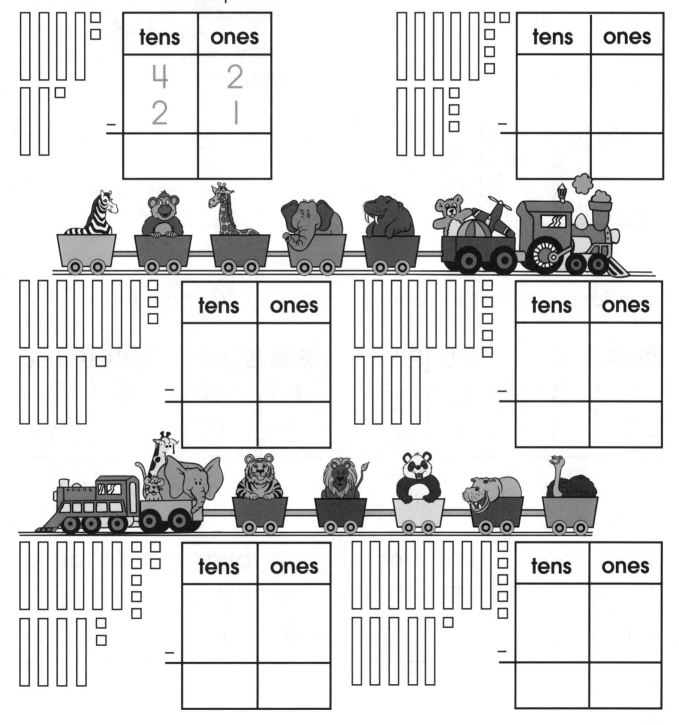

tens	ones
4	2
2	1

tens	ones

tens	ones

tens	ones

tens	ones

tens	ones

Your Total Solution for Math: Grade 2

© Carson-Dellosa • CD-704555

115

Name _____

Cookie Mania

There are 46 cookies.
Bill eats 22 cookies.
How many are left?

```
  46
- 22
────
```

1. Subtract the ones.

tens	ones
4	6
- 2	2
	4

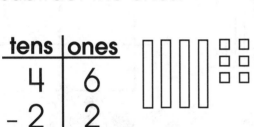

2. Subtract the tens.

tens	ones
4	6
- 2	2
2	4

Directions: Subtract the ones first. Then, subtract the tens.

tens	ones
7	8
- 2	5

tens	ones
5	9
- 3	6

tens	ones
8	3
- 6	1

tens	ones
6	7
- 4	3

tens	ones
9	7
- 1	4

tens	ones
5	4
- 3	0

tens	ones
4	2
- 3	1

tens	ones
2	8
- 1	8

Your Total Solution for Math: Grade 2

Name _____

Cookie Craze

Directions: Subtract to solve the problems. Circle the answers. Color the cookies with answers greater than 30.

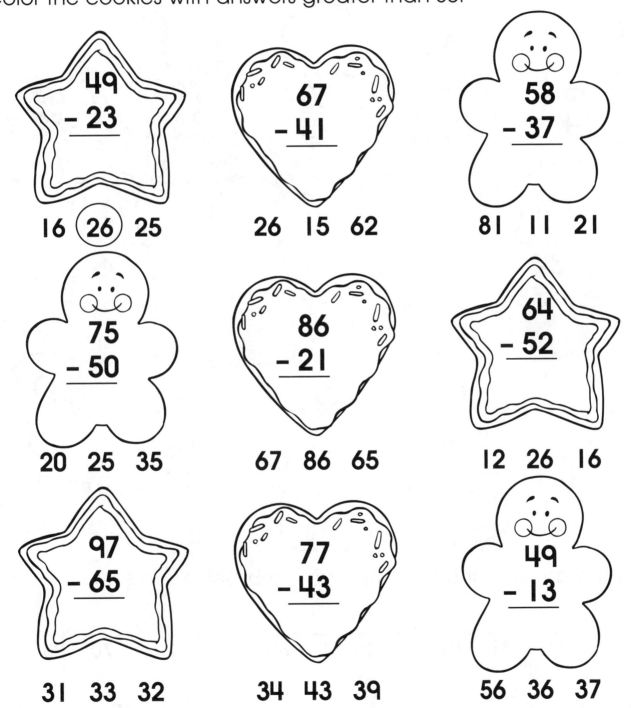

$$49 - 23$$

16   (26)   25

$$67 - 41$$

26   15   62

$$58 - 37$$

81   11   21

$$75 - 50$$

20   25   35

$$86 - 21$$

67   86   65

$$64 - 52$$

12   26   16

$$97 - 65$$

31   33   32

$$77 - 43$$

34   43   39

$$49 - 13$$

56   36   37

How's Your Pitch?

Directions: Solve the subtraction problems. Write each answer.

Use the answers and the letters on the baseballs to solve the code.

__ __ __ __ __ __ __ __ __ __ __
44 54 81 41 42 70 60 62 61 70 20

__ __ __ __ __ __ __ __ __ __ __ __ __ __!
41 70 32 61 60 54 21 60 31 41 32 82 60

Your Total Solution for Math: Grade 2

Prehistoric Problems

Directions: Solve the subtraction problems. Use the code to color the picture.

Code:
25 = blue   57 = green
31 = yellow   14 = orange
21 = brown   11 = red

$$47 - 22$$

$$52 - 21$$

$$25 - 11$$

$$62 - 31$$

$$77 - 20$$

$$51 - 40$$

$$69 - 12$$

$$98 - 41$$

$$55 - 34$$

Name _____

Two-Digit Addition: Regrouping

Addition is "putting together" or adding two or more numbers to find the sum. Regrouping is using **ten ones** to form **one ten**, **ten tens** to form **one 100**, **fifteen ones** to form **one ten** and **five ones**, and so on.

Directions: Study the examples. Follow the steps to add.

Example:

$$\begin{array}{r} 14 \\ +\ 8 \\ \hline \end{array}$$

Step 1:
Add the ones.

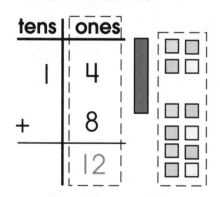

tens	ones
1	6
+ 3	7
5	3

Step 2:
Regroup the tens.

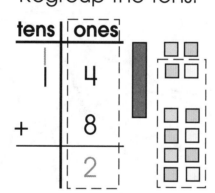

tens	ones
3	8
+ 5	3
9	1

Step 3:
Add the tens.

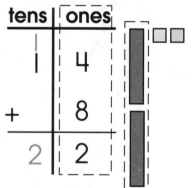

tens	ones
2	4
+ 4	7
7	1

$$\begin{array}{r} 28 \\ +17 \\ \hline \end{array} \qquad \begin{array}{r} 32 \\ +38 \\ \hline \end{array} \qquad \begin{array}{r} 54 \\ +25 \\ \hline \end{array} \qquad \begin{array}{r} 19 \\ +55 \\ \hline \end{array} \qquad \begin{array}{r} 44 \\ +48 \\ \hline \end{array} \qquad \begin{array}{r} 25 \\ +64 \\ \hline \end{array} \qquad \begin{array}{r} 29 \\ +33 \\ \hline \end{array} \qquad \begin{array}{r} 79 \\ +15 \\ \hline \end{array}$$

Your Total Solution for Math: Grade 2

Name _____

1+2

Two-Digit Addition: Regrouping

Directions: Add the total points scored in the game. Remember to add the ones, regroup, and then add the tens.

Example:

Total ___**85**___

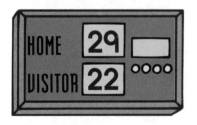

Total _____

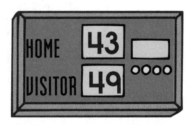

Total _____

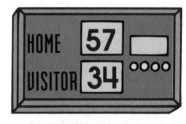

Total _____

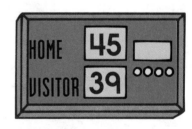

Total _____

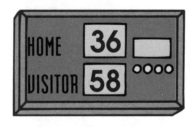

Total _____

Total _____

Total _____

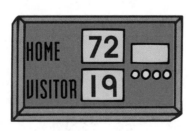

Total _____

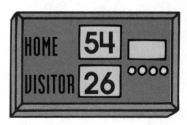

Total _____

Name _____

Two-Digit Addition

Directions: Add the ones.   Rename 15 as 10 + 5.   Add the tens.

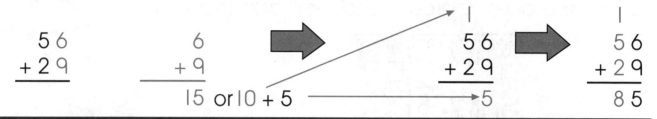

```
  5 6            6                        1              1
+ 2 9          + 9                      5 6            5 6
             ───────                  + 2 9          + 2 9
             15 or 10 + 5 ──────► 5   ─────          ─────
                                                     8 5
```

Directions: Add the ones.   Rename 12 as 10 + 2.   Add the tens.

```
  4 7            7                        1              1
+ 3 5          + 5                      4 7            4 7
             ───────                  + 3 5          + 3 5
             12 or 10 + 2 ──────► 2   ─────          ─────
                                                     8 2
```

Directions: Add.

Examples:

```
  4 5         1 3         4 8         6 9         5 4
+ 2 8       + 1 9       + 3 5       + 1 8       + 3 9
─────       ─────       ─────       ─────       ─────
  7 3         3 2
```

```
  4 4         3 7         2 8         7 3         6 6
+ 1 7       + 1 8       + 3 6       + 1 8       + 2 9
─────       ─────       ─────       ─────       ─────
```

```
  5 2         3 8         6 4         2 9         7 5
+ 3 9       + 4 7       + 1 8       + 4 5       + 1 7
─────       ─────       ─────       ─────       ─────
```

Your Total Solution for Math: Grade 2

Two-Digit Addition

Directions: Add the ones. Rename 11 as 10 + 1. Add the tens.

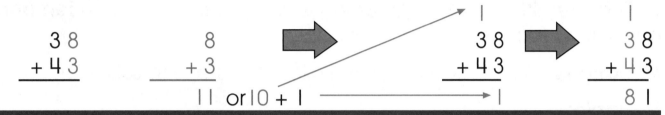

```
    3 8                8                          1                  1
  + 4 3              + 3                3 8                3 8
  _____          _____            + 4 3              + 4 3
                    1 1  or 10 + 1 ─────────→  1         _____
                                                            8 1
```

Directions: Add.

Example:

```
    1 7          2 6          4 7          6 8          3 7
  + 3 4        + 4 7        + 3 5        + 2 4        + 2 8
  _____      _____      _____      _____      _____
    5 1
```

```
    2 9          5 8          6 9          7 8          1 9
  + 4 8        + 2 7        + 1 7        + 1 3        + 4 4
  _____      _____      _____      _____      _____
```

```
    5 5          2 7          3 9          5 7          3 8
  + 2 8        + 3 5        + 5 2        + 2 7        + 3 6
  _____      _____      _____      _____      _____
```

```
    4 9          6 5          2 3          6 4          4 6
  + 4 3        + 1 8        + 1 8        + 1 8        + 3 9
  _____      _____      _____      _____      _____
```

```
    5 4          3 8          6 6          2 8          1 9
  + 2 7        + 4 4        + 2 6        + 3 4        + 5 6
  _____      _____      _____      _____      _____
```

Name _____

Two-Digit Subtraction: Regrouping

Subtraction is "taking away" or subtracting one number from another to find the difference. Regrouping is using **one ten** to form **ten ones**, **one 100** to form **ten tens**, and so on.

Directions: Study the examples. Follow the steps to subtract.

Example:
$$\begin{array}{r} 37 \\ -19 \\ \hline \end{array}$$

Step 1:
Regroup.

Step 2:
Subtract the ones.

Step 3:
Subtract the tens.

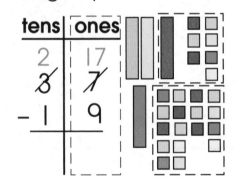

tens	ones
0	12
1	2
-	9
	3

tens	ones
2	14
3	4
- 1	6
1	8

tens	ones
3	15
4	5
- 2	9
1	6

$$\begin{array}{r} 28 \\ -19 \\ \hline \end{array} \quad \begin{array}{r} 46 \\ -18 \\ \hline \end{array} \quad \begin{array}{r} 12 \\ -\ 8 \\ \hline \end{array} \quad \begin{array}{r} 30 \\ -12 \\ \hline \end{array} \quad \begin{array}{r} 52 \\ -25 \\ \hline \end{array} \quad \begin{array}{r} 47 \\ -35 \\ \hline \end{array} \quad \begin{array}{r} 21 \\ -13 \\ \hline \end{array} \quad \begin{array}{r} 45 \\ -25 \\ \hline \end{array}$$

Your Total Solution for Math: Grade 2

Name _____

Two-Digit Subtraction: Regrouping

Directions: Study the steps for subtracting. Solve the problems using the steps.

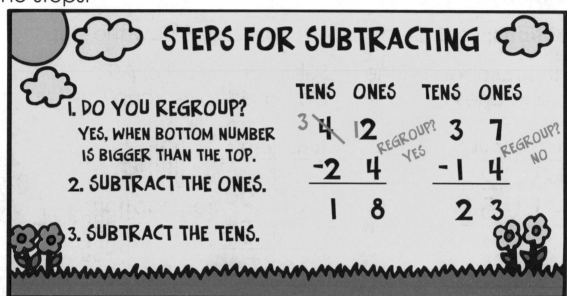

STEPS FOR SUBTRACTING

1. DO YOU REGROUP?
   YES, WHEN BOTTOM NUMBER IS BIGGER THAN THE TOP.
2. SUBTRACT THE ONES.
3. SUBTRACT THE TENS.

TENS	ONES		TENS	ONES
³4̶	12	REGROUP? YES	3	7	REGROUP? NO
-2	4		-1	4
1	8		2	3

tens	ones		tens	ones		tens	ones
4	7		6	4		5	3
- 2	8		- 3	4		- 3	9

$$
\begin{array}{r} 56 \\ -27 \\ \hline \end{array}
\qquad
\begin{array}{r} 83 \\ -47 \\ \hline \end{array}
\qquad
\begin{array}{r} 43 \\ -39 \\ \hline \end{array}
\qquad
\begin{array}{r} 75 \\ -53 \\ \hline \end{array}
\qquad
\begin{array}{r} 91 \\ -18 \\ \hline \end{array}
$$

$$
\begin{array}{r} 73 \\ -66 \\ \hline \end{array}
\qquad
\begin{array}{r} 35 \\ -14 \\ \hline \end{array}
\qquad
\begin{array}{r} 67 \\ -58 \\ \hline \end{array}
\qquad
\begin{array}{r} 26 \\ -7 \\ \hline \end{array}
\qquad
\begin{array}{r} 68 \\ -45 \\ \hline \end{array}
$$

Name _____

Seashell Subtraction

Ellen found 32 shells on the beach. She gave 15 shells to Cindy.
How many shells does Ellen have now?

Directions: Look at the problem below. Follow the steps to subtract.

Put the numbers on the
tens and ones table.

Subtract the ones. Ask:
Do I need to regroup?

regroup

32 = 2 tens and 12 ones.

Subtract the tens.

Ellen has 17 shells now.

Your Total Solution for Math: Grade 2

Name _____

Subtraction with Regrouping

Directions: Use manipulatives to find the difference.
Example:

tens	ones
4	14
5̶	4̶
− 1	7
3	7

tens	ones
3	3
− 1	5
☐	☐

tens	ones
6	1
− 3	3
☐	☐

tens	ones
2	7
− 1	6
☐	☐

tens	ones
4	2
− 2	4
☐	☐

tens	ones
5	2
− 2	6
☐	☐

tens	ones
9	4
− 4	8
☐	☐

tens	ones
7	7
− 3	4
☐	☐

tens	ones
6	5
− 2	6
☐	☐

Name _____

Two-Digit Subtraction

Directions: Rename 53 as 4 tens and 13 ones.

```
          4 13
   5 3      5̷ 3̷
 - 2 6    - 2 6
```

Subtract the ones.

```
   4 13
    5̷ 3̷
  - 2 6
      7
```

Subtract the tens.

```
   4 13
    5̷ 3̷
  - 2 6
    2 7
```

Rename 45 as 3 tens and 15 ones.

```
          3 15
   4 5      4̷ 5̷
 - 1 8    - 1 8
```

```
   3 15
    4̷ 5̷
  - 1 8
      7
```

```
   3 15
    4̷ 5̷
  - 1 8
    2 7
```

Directions: Subtract.

Examples:

```
  5 13        6 14
   6̷ 3̷         7̷ 4̷         4 7         5 2         6 4
 - 2 8      - 3 9       - 2 8       - 2 6       - 3 6
   3 5        3 5
```

```
  8 4          9 3         7 1         2 6         6 7
 - 4 7       - 5 6       - 2 3       - 1 8       - 4 8
```

```
  4 4          5 3         8 2         9 4         5 5
 - 2 8       - 3 7       - 4 6       - 6 6       - 3 9
```

```
  8 6          3 4         5 4         7 3         8 6
 - 5 8       - 1 8       - 2 9       - 5 9       - 6 9
```

Your Total Solution for Math: Grade 2

Two-Digit Subtraction

Directions: Rename 73 as 6 tens and 13 ones.

```
        6 13
  7 3    7̸ 3̸
- 4 8  - 4 8
```

Subtract the ones.

```
   6 13
   7̸ 3̸
 - 4 8
     5
```

Subtract the tens.

```
   6 13
   7̸ 3̸
 - 4 8
   2 5
```

Directions: Subtract.

Example:

```
   5 13
   6̸ 3̸
 - 4 8
   1 5
```

```
  8 3
- 4 5
```

```
  7 4
- 2 9
```

```
  9 4
- 4 8
```

```
  6 2
- 2 5
```

```
  4 5
- 2 7
```

```
  3 3
- 2 4
```

```
  2 4
-   8
```

```
  8 6
- 3 7
```

```
  7 2
- 4 8
```

```
  3 6
- 1 7
```

```
  2 6
- 1 8
```

```
  4 3
- 1 9
```

```
  6 3
- 4 8
```

```
  9 3
- 1 8
```

```
  8 2
- 2 6
```

```
  7 3
- 2 8
```

```
  9 5
- 6 9
```

```
  5 7
- 3 8
```

```
  4 1
- 2 5
```

```
  5 4
- 1 8
```

```
  6 1
- 3 4
```

```
  9 1
- 3 7
```

```
  8 1
- 4 4
```

```
  3 2
- 1 5
```

Name _____

Problem Solving

Directions: Solve each problem.

Example:

Dad cooks 23 potatoes.

He uses 19 potatoes in the potato salad.

How many potatoes are left?

Susan draws 32 butterflies.

She colored 15 of them brown.

How many butterflies does she have left to color?

A book has 66 pages.

Pedro reads 39 pages.

How many pages are left to read?

Jerry picks up 34 seashells.

He puts 15 of them in a box.

How many does he have left?

Beth buys 72 sheets of paper.

She uses 44 sheets for her school work.

How many sheets of paper are left?

Addition and Subtraction Review

Directions: Add.

4	8	9	7	5	6
+ 9	+ 6	+ 8	+ 6	+ 7	+ 5

9	5	7	9	8	7
+ 6	+ 8	+ 4	+ 9	+ 7	+ 9

30	20	45	52	60	83
+40	+30	+23	+23	+25	+15

Directions: Subtract.

16	15	13	12	11	17
− 7	− 9	− 4	− 7	− 9	− 8

18	17	16	15	14	16
− 9	− 9	− 8	− 8	− 7	− 9

40	60	85	73	96	54
−30	−10	−23	−41	−43	−44

Name _____

Review Two-Digit Addition

Directions: Add the ones.   Rename 12 as 10 + 2.   Add the tens.

$$
\begin{array}{r} 64 \\ +28 \\ \hline \end{array}
\qquad
\begin{array}{r} 4 \\ +8 \\ \hline 12 \text{ or } 10+2 \end{array}
\qquad
\begin{array}{r} {}^{1} \\ 64 \\ +28 \\ \hline 2 \end{array}
\qquad
\begin{array}{r} {}^{1} \\ 64 \\ +28 \\ \hline 92 \end{array}
$$

Directions: Add.

Example:

$$
\begin{array}{r} 28 \\ +19 \\ \hline 47 \end{array}
\qquad
\begin{array}{r} 34 \\ +49 \\ \hline \end{array}
\qquad
\begin{array}{r} 25 \\ +16 \\ \hline \end{array}
\qquad
\begin{array}{r} 46 \\ +29 \\ \hline \end{array}
\qquad
\begin{array}{r} 54 \\ +39 \\ \hline \end{array}
$$

$$
\begin{array}{r} 16 \\ +39 \\ \hline \end{array}
\qquad
\begin{array}{r} 64 \\ +28 \\ \hline \end{array}
\qquad
\begin{array}{r} 58 \\ +24 \\ \hline \end{array}
\qquad
\begin{array}{r} 39 \\ +17 \\ \hline \end{array}
\qquad
\begin{array}{r} 34 \\ +19 \\ \hline \end{array}
$$

$$
\begin{array}{r} 57 \\ +39 \\ \hline \end{array}
\qquad
\begin{array}{r} 14 \\ +48 \\ \hline \end{array}
\qquad
\begin{array}{r} 37 \\ +39 \\ \hline \end{array}
\qquad
\begin{array}{r} 61 \\ +19 \\ \hline \end{array}
\qquad
\begin{array}{r} 29 \\ +44 \\ \hline \end{array}
$$

$$
\begin{array}{r} 17 \\ +35 \\ \hline \end{array}
\qquad
\begin{array}{r} 39 \\ +14 \\ \hline \end{array}
\qquad
\begin{array}{r} 44 \\ +37 \\ \hline \end{array}
\qquad
\begin{array}{r} 25 \\ +49 \\ \hline \end{array}
\qquad
\begin{array}{r} 18 \\ +18 \\ \hline \end{array}
$$

$$
\begin{array}{r} 26 \\ +48 \\ \hline \end{array}
\qquad
\begin{array}{r} 39 \\ +27 \\ \hline \end{array}
\qquad
\begin{array}{r} 14 \\ +27 \\ \hline \end{array}
\qquad
\begin{array}{r} 65 \\ +25 \\ \hline \end{array}
\qquad
\begin{array}{r} 59 \\ +18 \\ \hline \end{array}
$$

Your Total Solution for Math: Grade 2

Keep on Truckin'

Directions: Write each sum. Connect the sums of 83 to make a road for the truck.

17 +66	48 +26	42 +19

28	64	26	58	17	65
+38	+19	+57	+25	+75	+29

37	48	58	65	38	39
+39	+35	+37	+16	+25	+59

59	55	39
+27	+28	+44

Name _____

Review Two-Digit Subtraction

Directions: Rename 61 as 5 tens and 11 ones.

```
        5 11
  6 1    6̸ 1̸
- 4 3  - 4 3
```

Subtract the ones.

```
  5 11
  6̸ 1̸
- 4 3
    8
```

Subtract the tens.

```
  5 11
  6̸ 1̸
- 4 3
  1 8
```

Directions: Subtract.

Example:

```
  3 17
  4̸ 7̸
- 2 8
  1 9
```

```
  7 3
- 4 8
```

```
  8 4
- 6 6
```

```
  9 5
- 1 8
```

```
  6 4
- 2 9
```

```
  5 6
- 3 8
```

```
  3 1
- 1 5
```

```
  2 5
- 1 7
```

```
  3 3
- 1 9
```

```
  4 6
- 2 9
```

```
  9 3
- 6 4
```

```
  8 2
- 5 5
```

```
  7 2
- 1 4
```

```
  4 5
- 2 8
```

```
  6 1
- 2 3
```

```
  5 1
- 4 4
```

```
  6 2
- 4 8
```

```
  3 7
- 1 9
```

```
  5 0
- 3 2
```

```
  8 3
- 4 7
```

```
  9 2
- 7 3
```

```
  8 2
- 7 5
```

```
  7 6
- 3 8
```

```
  4 7
- 2 9
```

```
  7 4
- 3 9
```

Your Total Solution for Math: Grade 2

Review Two-Digit Subtraction

Directions: Subtract.

$$\begin{array}{r} 85 \\ -16 \\ \hline \end{array} \qquad \begin{array}{r} 93 \\ -48 \\ \hline \end{array} \qquad \begin{array}{r} 72 \\ -35 \\ \hline \end{array} \qquad \begin{array}{r} 63 \\ -27 \\ \hline \end{array} \qquad \begin{array}{r} 43 \\ -38 \\ \hline \end{array}$$

$$\begin{array}{r} 56 \\ -29 \\ \hline \end{array} \qquad \begin{array}{r} 75 \\ -49 \\ \hline \end{array} \qquad \begin{array}{r} 84 \\ -38 \\ \hline \end{array} \qquad \begin{array}{r} 91 \\ -65 \\ \hline \end{array} \qquad \begin{array}{r} 37 \\ -18 \\ \hline \end{array}$$

$$\begin{array}{r} 21 \\ -14 \\ \hline \end{array} \qquad \begin{array}{r} 35 \\ -18 \\ \hline \end{array} \qquad \begin{array}{r} 42 \\ -29 \\ \hline \end{array} \qquad \begin{array}{r} 72 \\ -47 \\ \hline \end{array} \qquad \begin{array}{r} 81 \\ -54 \\ \hline \end{array}$$

$$\begin{array}{r} 64 \\ -38 \\ \hline \end{array} \qquad \begin{array}{r} 53 \\ -28 \\ \hline \end{array} \qquad \begin{array}{r} 94 \\ -57 \\ \hline \end{array} \qquad \begin{array}{r} 48 \\ -39 \\ \hline \end{array} \qquad \begin{array}{r} 23 \\ -18 \\ \hline \end{array}$$

$$\begin{array}{r} 74 \\ -58 \\ \hline \end{array} \qquad \begin{array}{r} 83 \\ -36 \\ \hline \end{array} \qquad \begin{array}{r} 62 \\ -26 \\ \hline \end{array} \qquad \begin{array}{r} 54 \\ -28 \\ \hline \end{array} \qquad \begin{array}{r} 32 \\ -17 \\ \hline \end{array}$$

Name _____

Go "Fore" It

Directions: Add or subtract using regrouping.

tens	ones
2	15
~~3~~	5
-2	7
	8

$$\begin{array}{r} 35 \\ +27 \\ \hline \end{array}$$

$$\begin{array}{r} 40 \\ -16 \\ \hline \end{array}$$

$$\begin{array}{r} 56 \\ -27 \\ \hline \end{array}$$

$$\begin{array}{r} 93 \\ -39 \\ \hline \end{array}$$

$$\begin{array}{r} 44 \\ +28 \\ \hline \end{array}$$

$$\begin{array}{r} 42 \\ -14 \\ \hline \end{array}$$

$$\begin{array}{r} 33 \\ +18 \\ \hline \end{array}$$

$$\begin{array}{r} 97 \\ -48 \\ \hline \end{array}$$

$$\begin{array}{r} 73 \\ -24 \\ \hline \end{array}$$

$$\begin{array}{r} 56 \\ -17 \\ \hline \end{array}$$

$$\begin{array}{r} 68 \\ -49 \\ \hline \end{array}$$

$$\begin{array}{r} 49 \\ +32 \\ \hline \end{array}$$

$$\begin{array}{r} 77 \\ -68 \\ \hline \end{array}$$

$$\begin{array}{r} 27 \\ +19 \\ \hline \end{array}$$

Your Total Solution for Math: Grade 2

Name _____

Monster Math

Directions: Add or subtract using regrouping.

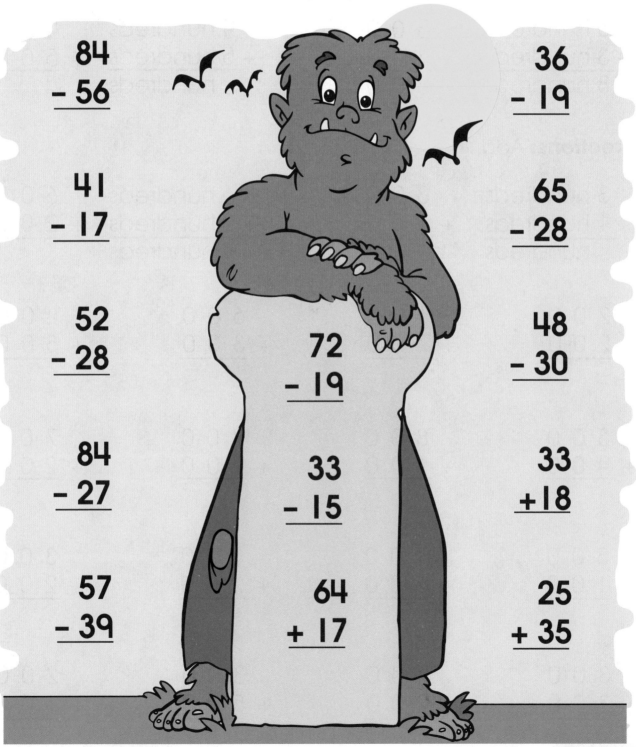

$$\begin{array}{r} 84 \\ -\ 56 \\ \hline \end{array}$$

$$\begin{array}{r} 41 \\ -\ 17 \\ \hline \end{array}$$

$$\begin{array}{r} 52 \\ -\ 28 \\ \hline \end{array}$$

$$\begin{array}{r} 84 \\ -\ 27 \\ \hline \end{array}$$

$$\begin{array}{r} 57 \\ -\ 39 \\ \hline \end{array}$$

$$\begin{array}{r} 72 \\ -\ 19 \\ \hline \end{array}$$

$$\begin{array}{r} 33 \\ -\ 15 \\ \hline \end{array}$$

$$\begin{array}{r} 64 \\ +\ 17 \\ \hline \end{array}$$

$$\begin{array}{r} 36 \\ -\ 19 \\ \hline \end{array}$$

$$\begin{array}{r} 65 \\ -\ 28 \\ \hline \end{array}$$

$$\begin{array}{r} 48 \\ -\ 30 \\ \hline \end{array}$$

$$\begin{array}{r} 33 \\ +18 \\ \hline \end{array}$$

$$\begin{array}{r} 25 \\ +\ 35 \\ \hline \end{array}$$

Name _____

Adding Hundreds

Examples:

5 hundreds	5 0 0	4 hundreds	4 0 0
+ 3 hundreds	+ 3 0 0	+ 5 hundreds	+ 5 0 0
8 hundreds	8 0 0	9 hundreds	900

Directions: Add.

3 hundreds	3 0 0	6 hundreds	6 0 0
+ 1 hundreds	+ 1 0 0	+ 2 hundreds	+ 2 0 0
4 hundreds	400	hundreds	

```
  2 0 0       1 0 0       6 0 0       4 0 0
+ 2 0 0     + 7 0 0     + 3 0 0     + 5 0 0

  3 0 0       8 0 0       4 0 0       7 0 0
+ 4 0 0     + 1 0 0     + 4 0 0     + 2 0 0

  5 0 0       1 0 0       5 0 0       3 0 0
+ 1 0 0     + 6 0 0     + 2 0 0     + 2 0 0

  3 0 0       4 0 0       3 0 0       2 0 0
+ 3 0 0     + 2 0 0     + 5 0 0     + 1 0 0
```

Your Total Solution for Math: Grade 2

Problem Solving

Directions: Solve each problem.

Example:

Ria packed 300 boxes.

Melvin packed 200 boxes.

How many boxes did Ria and Melvin pack?

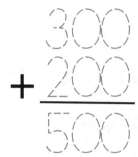

$$+ \frac{300}{\underline{200}} \atop 500$$

Santo typed 500 letters.

Hale typed 400 letters.

How many letters did they type?

Paula used 100 paper clips.

Milton used 600 paper clips.

How many paper clips did they use?

The grocery store sold 400 red apples.

The grocery store also sold 100 yellow apples.

How many apples did the grocery store sell in all?

Miles worked 200 days.

Julia worked 500 days.

How many days did they work?

Name _____

Three-Digit Addition

```
   2 4 5              2 4 5              2 4 5
 + 2 5 3            + 2 5 3            + 2 5 3
       8                9 8            4 9 8
```

Directions: Add.

Example:

```
   7 4 5              6 2 3
 +   2 3            + 1 5 6
   7 6 8
```

— Add the ones.
— Add the tens.
— Add the hundreds.

— Add the ones.
— Add the tens.
— Add the hundreds.

```
   4 1 5        5 6 6        3 7 3        1 6 0
 + 3 4 2      +   3 3      + 2 2 1      + 3 3 4
```

```
   8 3 5        6 4 2        2 8 7        7 2 3
 +   4 2      + 2 5 1      + 4 1 2      +   4 5
```

```
   1 3 3        4 5 4        3 1 4        6 5 4
 + 5 2 2      + 3 2 4      + 6 0 2      + 2 3 5
```

Your Total Solution for Math: Grade 2

Problem Solving

Directions: Solve each problem.

Example:

Gene collected 342 rocks.

Lester collected 201 rocks.

How many rocks did they collect?

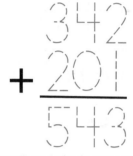

Tina jumped the rope 403 times.

Henry jumped the rope 426 times.

How many times did they jump?

There are 210 people wearing blue hats.

There are 432 people wearing red hats.

How many hats in all?

Asta used 135 paper plates.

Clyde used 143 paper plates.

How many paper plates did they use in all?

Aunt Mary had 536 dollars.

Uncle Lewis had 423 dollars.

How many dollars did they have in all?

Name _____

Subtracting Hundreds

8 hundreds	8 0 0	6 hundreds	6 0 0
- 3 hundreds	- 3 0 0	- 2 hundreds	- 2 0 0
5 hundreds	5 0 0	4 hundreds	4̶0̶0̶

Directions: Subtract.

Example:

9 hundreds	9 0 0	3 hundreds	3 0 0
- 7 hundreds	- 7 0 0	- 1 hundreds	- 1 0 0
2̶ hundreds	2̶0̶0̶	hundreds	

$$\begin{array}{r} 7\ 0\ 0 \\ -\ 3\ 0\ 0 \\ \hline \end{array} \qquad \begin{array}{r} 5\ 0\ 0 \\ -\ 4\ 0\ 0 \\ \hline \end{array} \qquad \begin{array}{r} 9\ 0\ 0 \\ -\ 4\ 0\ 0 \\ \hline \end{array} \qquad \begin{array}{r} 8\ 0\ 0 \\ -\ 5\ 0\ 0 \\ \hline \end{array}$$

$$\begin{array}{r} 6\ 0\ 0 \\ -\ 5\ 0\ 0 \\ \hline \end{array} \qquad \begin{array}{r} 3\ 0\ 0 \\ -\ 2\ 0\ 0 \\ \hline \end{array} \qquad \begin{array}{r} 5\ 0\ 0 \\ -\ 1\ 0\ 0 \\ \hline \end{array} \qquad \begin{array}{r} 4\ 0\ 0 \\ -\ 2\ 0\ 0 \\ \hline \end{array}$$

$$\begin{array}{r} 9\ 0\ 0 \\ -\ 1\ 0\ 0 \\ \hline \end{array} \qquad \begin{array}{r} 8\ 0\ 0 \\ -\ 4\ 0\ 0 \\ \hline \end{array} \qquad \begin{array}{r} 6\ 0\ 0 \\ -\ 2\ 0\ 0 \\ \hline \end{array} \qquad \begin{array}{r} 5\ 0\ 0 \\ -\ 3\ 0\ 0 \\ \hline \end{array}$$

$$\begin{array}{r} 4\ 0\ 0 \\ -\ 1\ 0\ 0 \\ \hline \end{array} \qquad \begin{array}{r} 7\ 0\ 0 \\ -\ 6\ 0\ 0 \\ \hline \end{array} \qquad \begin{array}{r} 8\ 0\ 0 \\ -\ 2\ 0\ 0 \\ \hline \end{array} \qquad \begin{array}{r} 9\ 0\ 0 \\ -\ 6\ 0\ 0 \\ \hline \end{array}$$

Your Total Solution for Math: Grade 2

Problem Solving

Directions: Solve each problem.

Example:

There were 400 apples in a box.

Jesse took 100 apples from the box.

How many apples are still in the box?

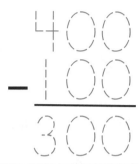

$$\begin{array}{r} 400 \\ -\ 100 \\ \hline 300 \end{array}$$

Tommy bought 300 golf balls.

He gave Irene 200 golf balls.

How many golf balls does he have left?

The black horse ran 900 feet.

The brown horse ran 700 feet.

How many more feet did the black horse run?

The paint store has 800 gallons of paint.

It sells 300 gallons of paint.

How many gallons of paint are left?

There are 700 children.

There are 200 boys.

How many girls are there?

Name _____

Three-Digit Subtraction

Directions: Subtract the ones.

```
  7 4 6
- 4 2 4
      2
```

Subtract the tens.

```
  7 4 6
- 4 2 4
    2 2
```

Subtract the hundreds.

```
  7 4 6
- 4 2 2
  3 2 2
```

Directions: Subtract.

Example:

```
  8 7 9
-   4 6
  8 3 3
```

└── Subtract the ones.
└── Subtract the tens.
└── Subtract the hundreds.

```
  5 8 6
- 1 4 2
```

└── Subtract the ones.
└── Subtract the tens.
└── Subtract the hundreds.

```
  6 3 5          4 7 8          3 3 8          9 5 7
- 4 2 3        - 2 4 1        -   2 7        - 7 3 4
```

```
  2 9 7          8 4 6          7 6 9          6 5 3
- 1 4 5        - 3 2 5        - 5 1 4        - 1 4 2
```

```
  5 6 9          3 6 5          8 1 8          9 3 6
- 3 3 3        - 2 1 3        - 6 1 8        - 4 2 4
```

Name _____

Problem Solving

Directions: Solve each problem.

Example:

There were 787 bales of hay.

Glenda fed the cows 535 bales.

How many bales of hay are left?

$$\begin{array}{r} 787 \\ -\ 535 \\ \hline 252 \end{array}$$

There are 673 bolts in a box.

Maria took 341 bolts out of the box.

How many bolts are left in the box?

The secretary types 459 letters.

138 of the letters were mailed.

How many letters are left?

Mr. Jones had 569 dollars.

He spent 203 dollars.

How many dollars does he have left?

There are 342 riding horses in the rodeo.

There are 132 bucking horses in the rodeo.

How many more riding horses are there?

Name _____

Review: Three-Digit Addition

Directions: Add.

Examples:

```
   3 4 0        7 5 4        8 2 6        6 3 2
 + 2 2 5      +   3 2      +     3      + 3 2 2
   5 6 5        7 8 6
```

```
   1 9 8        4 5 6        5 4 1        2 7 3
 + 2 0 0      +   3 1      + 3 3 3      + 4 1 5
```

```
   9 0 0        8 4 7        7 2 1        4 0 2
 +   3 4      + 1 3 1      + 1 7 6      + 3 8 3
```

```
   1 5 6        6 4 4        2 1 5        3 7 2
 + 4 2 3      + 2 5 1      + 5 4 2      + 4 1 7
```

```
   5 1 8        7 8 3        6 8 4        7 1 0
 + 3 5 1      +     5      +   1 4      + 2 6 0
```

Your Total Solution for Math: Grade 2

Review: Three-Digit Subtraction

Directions: Subtract.

Example:

```
  8 5 6        4 3 2        5 9 8        7 6 9
- 3 5 2      -   2 1      - 4 1 6      - 3 4 5
  5 0 4        4 1 1
```

```
  3 1 9        9 5 4        2 7 5        6 4 3
-     6      - 7 3 1      -     3      - 3 1 3
```

```
  7 7 5        8 3 4        9 4 2        4 7 8
- 2 6 1      -   1 2      - 1 1 1      - 3 2 4
```

```
  5 6 2        4 4 4        3 8 5        7 5 4
- 4 3 1      - 2 1 2      - 1 5 2      -     3
```

```
  8 6 8        9 4 3        6 8 9        5 7 7
- 2 3 4      - 8 4 3      - 4 1 7      -   3 7
```

Name _____

Multiplication

Multiplication is a short way to find the sum of adding the same number a certain amount of times. For example, 7 x 4 = 28 instead of 7 + 7 + 7 + 7 = 28.

Directions: Study the example. Solve the problems.

Example:

3 + 3 + 3 = 9
3 threes = 9
3 x 3 = 9

7 + 7 = ____
2 sevens = ____
2 x 7 = ____

4 + 4 + 4 + 4 = ____
4 fours = ____
4 x ____ = ____

5 + 5 = ____
2 fives = ____
2 x ____ = ____

2 + 2 + 2 + 2 = ____
4 twos = ____
4 x ____ = ____

6 + 6 = ____
2 sixes = ____
2 x ____ = ____

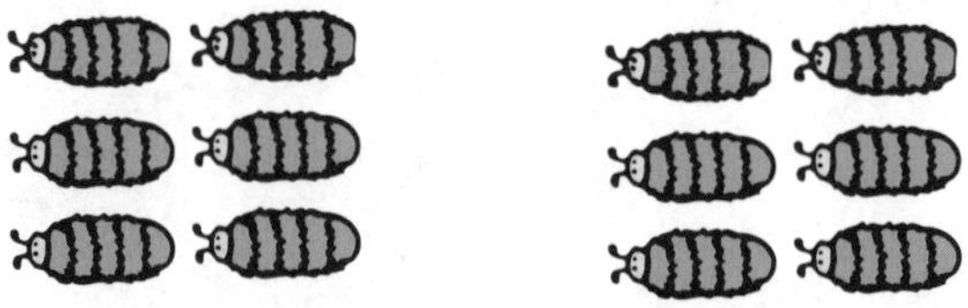

© Carson-Dellosa • CD-704555

Multiplication

Multiplication is repeated addition.

Directions: Draw a picture for each problem. Then, write the missing numbers.

Example:
Draw 2 groups of three apples.

3 + 3 = 6

or   2 x 3 = 6

Draw 3 groups of four hearts.	Draw 2 groups of five boxes.
 4 + 4 + 4 = ____ or 3 x ____ = ____	5 + ____ = ____ or 2 x ____ = ____

Draw 6 groups of two circles.

2 + ____ + ____ + ____ + ____ + ____ = ____

or   6 x ____ = ____

Draw 7 groups of three triangles.

3 + ____ + ____ + ____ + ____ + ____ + ____ = ____

or   ____ x ____ = ____

Name _____

Multiplication

Directions: Study the example. Draw the groups and write the total.

Example:
3x2
2+2+2   =   → 6 ____

(•• •• ••)

3x4

___ + ___ + ___ = _____

2x5

____ + ____ = _____

5x3

___ + ___ + ___ + ___ + ___ = _____

Your Total Solution for Math: Grade 2

Multiplication

Directions: Solve the problems.

Multiplication saves time.
It's faster than addition!

$9 + 9 =$ _____

2 nines = _____

$2 \times 9 =$ _____

$7 + 7 =$ _____

2 sevens = _____

$2 \times$ _____ $=$ _____

$4 + 4 + 4 + 4 =$ _____

_____ fours = _____

_____ $\times 4 =$ _____

$8 + 8 + 8 + 8 + 8 =$ _____

_____ eights = _____

_____ $\times 8 =$ _____

$5 + 5 + 5 =$ _____

_____ fives = _____

_____ $\times 5 =$ _____

$9 + 9 =$ _____

_____ nines = _____

_____ $\times 9 =$ _____

$6 + 6 + 6 =$ _____

_____ sixes = _____

_____ $\times 6 =$ _____

$3 + 3 =$ _____

_____ threes = _____

_____ $\times 3 =$ _____

$7 + 7 + 7 + 7 =$ _____

_____ sevens = _____

_____ $\times 7 =$ _____

$2 + 2 =$ _____

_____ twos = _____

_____ $\times 2 =$ _____

Name _____

Multiplication

Directions: Use the code to color the fish.

If the answer is:

 6, color it **red**.

 12, color it **orange**.

 16, color it **blue**.

 27, color it **brown**.

 8, color it yellow.

 15, color it **green**.

 18, color it **purple**.

© Carson-Dellosa • CD-704555

Your Total Solution for Math: Grade 2

Name _____

Problem Solving

Directions: Tell if you add, subtract, or multiply. Then, write the answers.

There were 12 frogs sitting on a log by a pond, but 3 frogs hopped away. How many frogs were left?

_____ _____ frogs

There are 9 flowers growing by the pond. Each flower has 2 leaves. How many leaves are there?

_____ _____ leaves

A tree had 7 squirrels playing in it. Then, 8 more came along. How many squirrels are there in all?

_____ _____ squirrels

There were 27 birds living in the trees around the pond, but 9 flew away. How many birds are left?

_____ _____ birds

Name _____

Circle

A **circle** is a shape that is round. This is a circle: ◯

Directions: Find the circles and draw squares around them.

Directions: Trace the word. Then, write the word.

circle

Your Total Solution for Math: Grade 2

Name _____

Square

A **square** is a shape with four corners and four sides of the same length. This is a square:

Directions: Find the squares and draw circles around them.

Directions: Trace the word. Then, write the word.

Name _____

Rectangle

A **rectangle** is a shape with four corners and four sides. The sides opposite each other are the same length. This is a rectangle: ▭

Directions: Find the rectangles and draw circles around them.

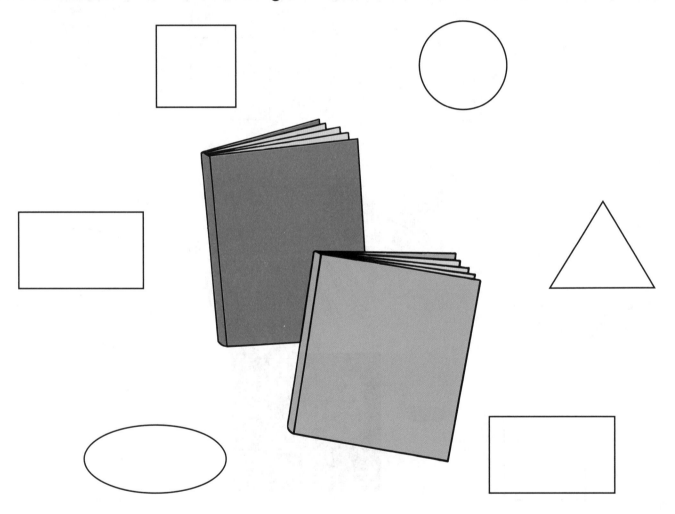

Directions: Trace the word. Then, write the word.

rectangle _____

Your Total Solution for Math: Grade 2

Triangle

A **triangle** is a shape with three corners and three sides.

This is a triangle: △

Directions: Find the triangles and draw circles around them.

Directions: Trace the word. Then, write the word.

Name _____

Oval and Rhombus

An **oval** is egg-shaped. This is an oval: ○

A **rhombus** is a shape with four sides of the same length. Its corners form points at the top, sides, and bottom. This is a rhombus: ◇

Directions: Find the ovals. Color them **red**.
Find the rhombuses. Color them **blue**.

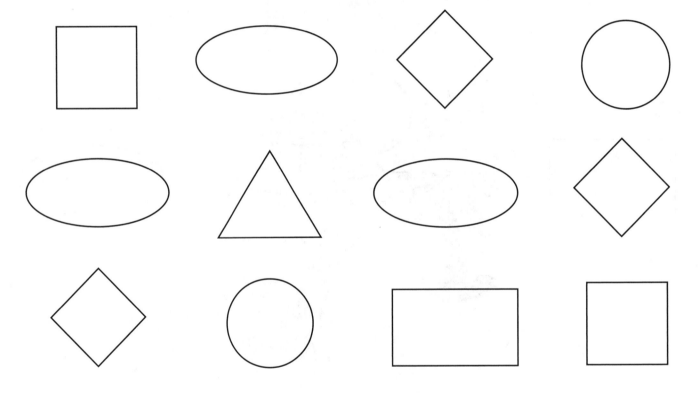

Directions: Trace the words. Then, write the words.

oval _____

rhombus _____

© Carson-Dellosa • CD-704555
Your Total Solution for Math: Grade 2

Geometry

Geometry is mathematics that has to do with lines and shapes.

Directions: Color the shapes.

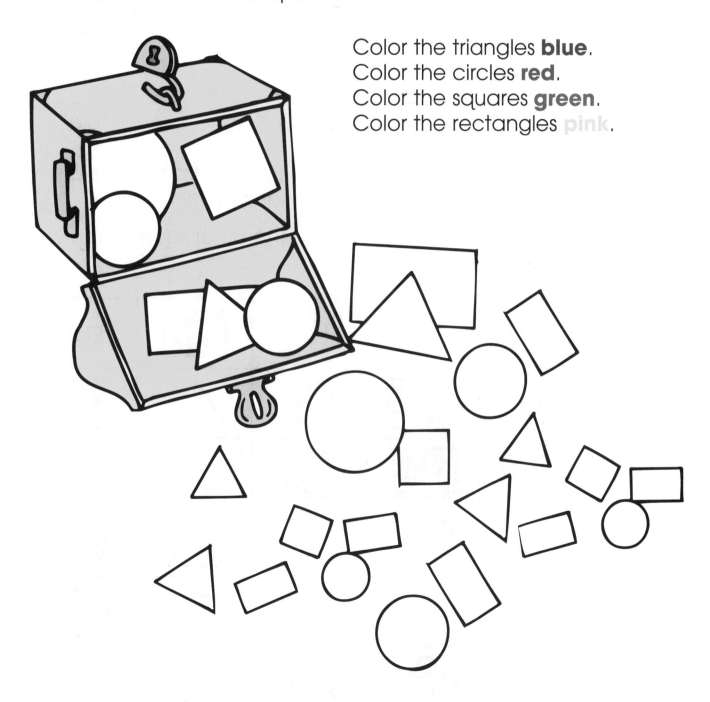

Color the triangles **blue**.
Color the circles **red**.
Color the squares **green**.
Color the rectangles pink.

Name _____

Shapes

Directions: Some shapes have sides. How many sides does each shape below have? Write the number of sides inside each shape.

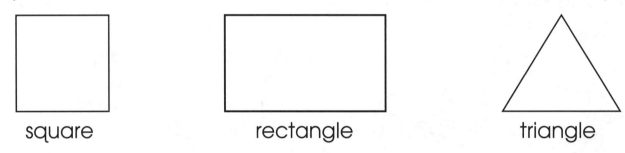

square   rectangle   triangle

Directions: Help Robbie get to his space car by tracing the path that has only squares, rectangles, and triangles.

Hint: You may want to draw an **X** on all the other shapes. This will help you see the path more clearly.

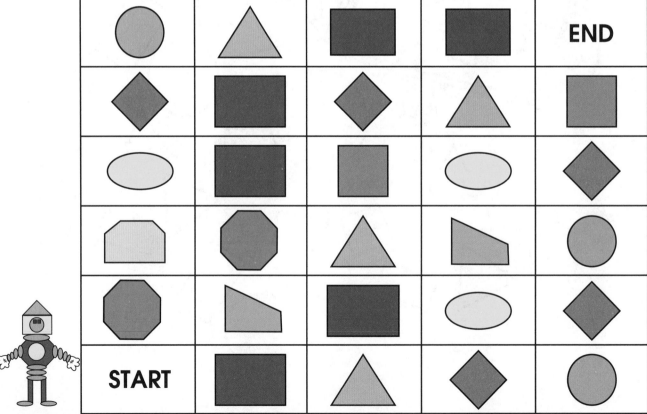

Shapes

Directions: Look at the grid below. All the shapes have straight sides, like a square.

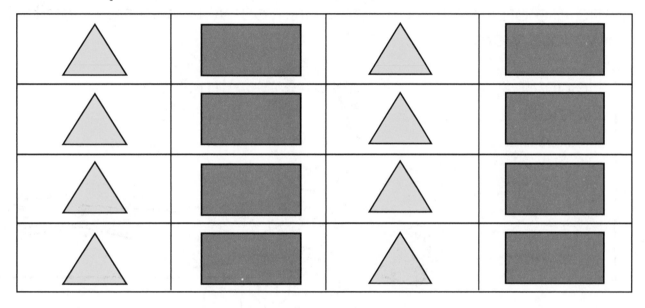

Directions: Now, make your own pattern grid. Use only shapes with straight sides like the grid above. The grid has been started for you.

Name _____

How Big Are You?

Directions: How big are you? **Estimate**, or guess, how long some of your body parts are. Write your estimates below. Then, have a friend use an inch ruler to measure you. Write the numbers below. How close were your estimates?

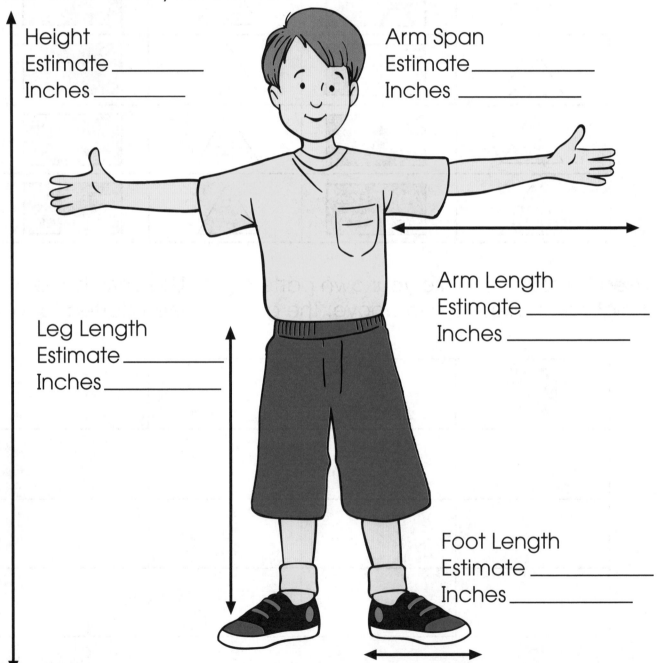

Height
Estimate_____
Inches_____

Arm Span
Estimate_____
Inches _____

Arm Length
Estimate_____
Inches_____

Leg Length
Estimate_____
Inches_____

Foot Length
Estimate_____
Inches_____

Measurement: Inches

Directions: Cut out the ruler. Measure each object to the nearest inch.

 _____ inches

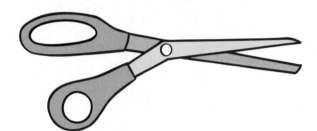 _____ inches

 _____ inch

Directions: Measure objects around your house. Write the measurement to the nearest inch.

can of soup _____ inches

pen _____ inches

toothbrush _____ inches

paper clip _____ inches

small toy _____ inches

cut out

8

7

6

5

4

3

2

1

Name _____

Measurement: Inches

Directions: Use the ruler from pg. 163 to measure the fish to the nearest inch.

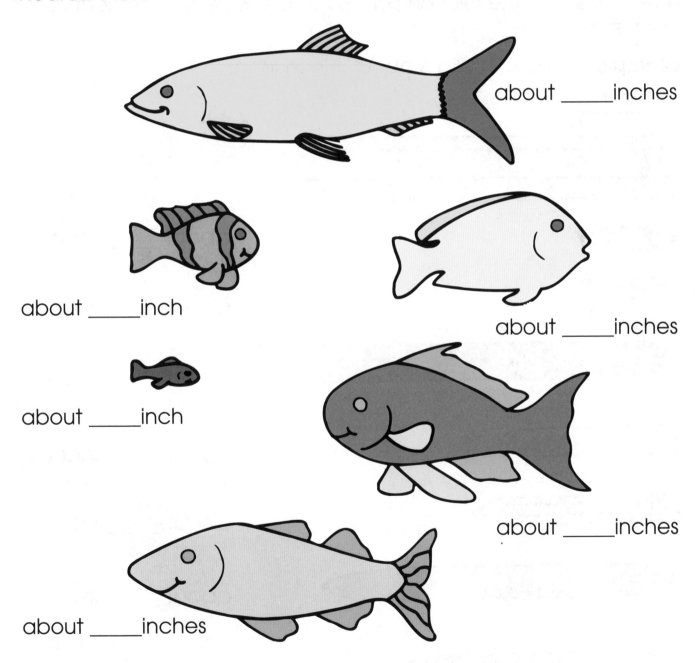

about _____ inches

about _____ inch

about _____ inches

about _____ inch

about _____ inches

about _____ inches

Name _____

Measurement: Inches

An **inch** is a unit of length in the standard measurement system.

Directions: Use the ruler on pg. 163 to measure each object to the nearest inch.

Example: The paper clip is about 1 inch long.

1 inch

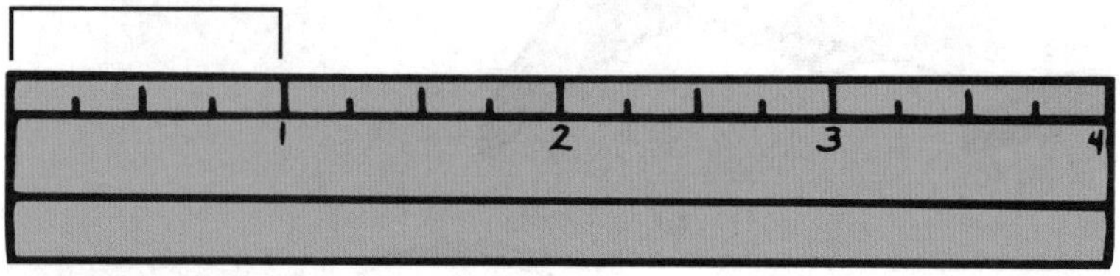

about __1__ inch

about _____ inch

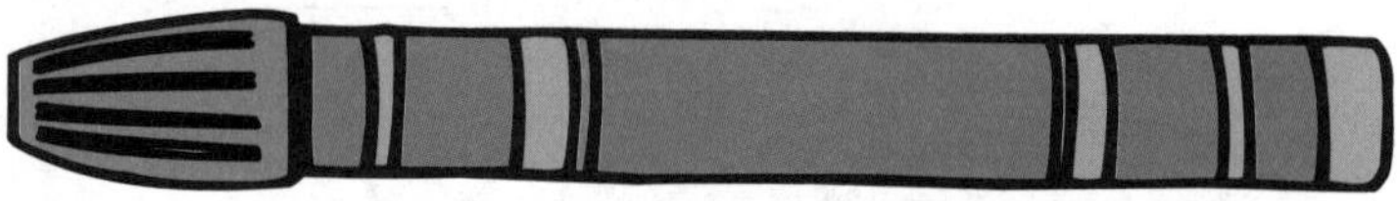

about _____ inches

about _____ inches

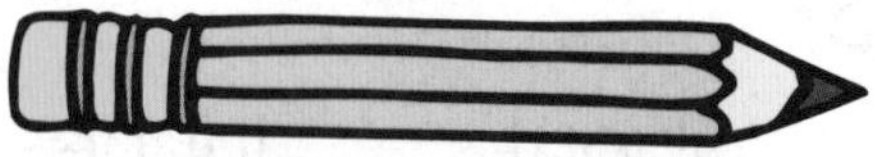

about _____ inches

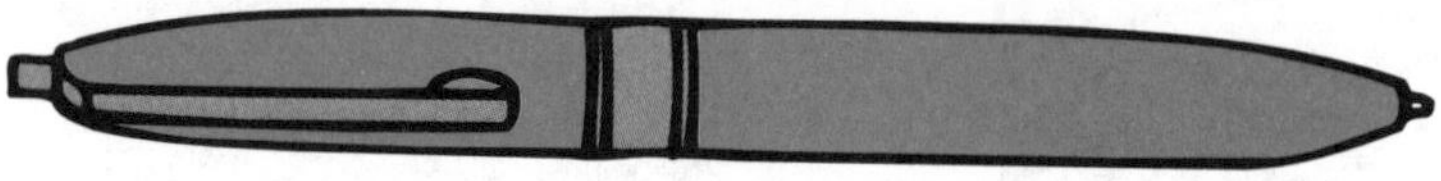

about _____ inches

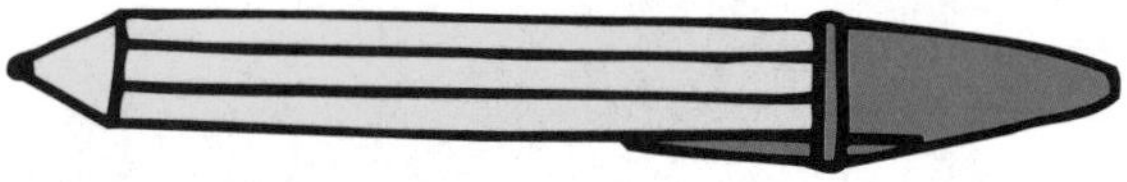

about _____ inches

Your Total Solution for Math: Grade 2

Measuring Monkeys

Directions: Use the inch ruler on pg. 163 to measure the length of each rope. Write the answer in each blank.

Name _____

Measurement: Centimeters

A **centimeter** is a unit of length in the metric system. There are 2.54 centimeters in an inch.

Directions: Use a centimeter ruler to measure the crayons to the nearest centimeter.

Example: The first crayon is about 7 centimeters long.

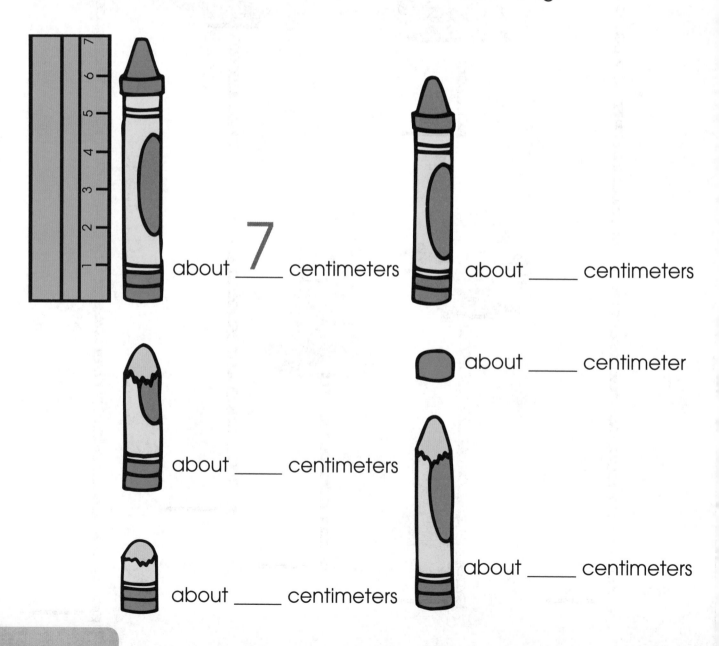

about __7__ centimeters

about _____ centimeters

about _____ centimeter

about _____ centimeters

about _____ centimeters

about _____ centimeters

Name _____

Measurement: Centimeters

Directions: The giraffe is about 8 centimeters high. How many centimeters (cm) high are the trees? Write your answers in the blanks.

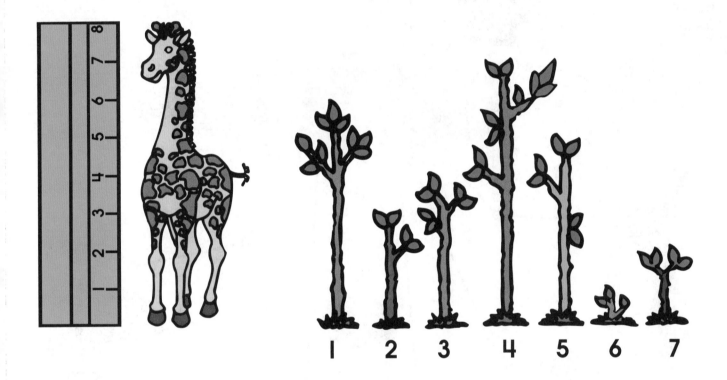

1. _____ cm   2. _____ cm   3. _____ cm

4. _____ cm   5. _____ cm   6. _____ cm   7. _____ cm

Name _____

Trip to the Watering Hole

Directions: Use a centimeter ruler to measure the distance each animal has to travel to reach the watering hole. Write the answer in each blank.

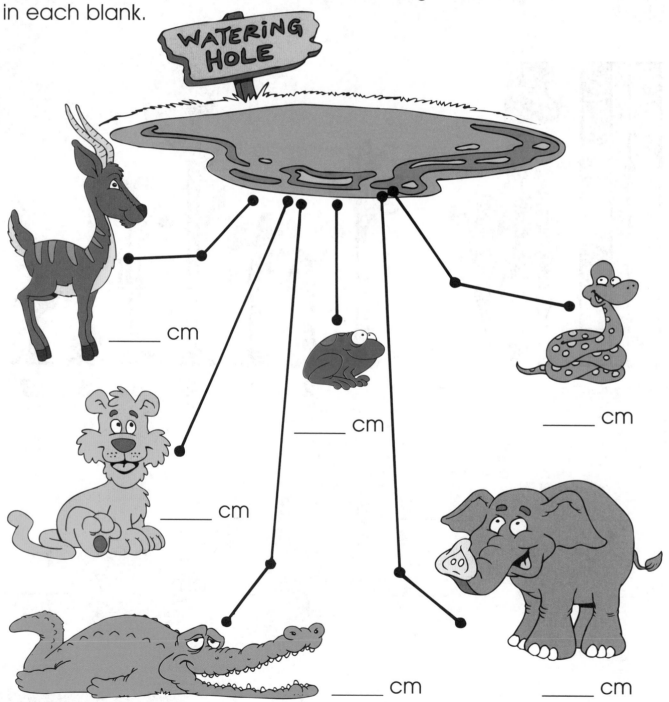

_____ cm

_____ cm

_____ cm

_____ cm

_____ cm

_____ cm

Your Total Solution for Math: Grade 2

Centimeter Sharpening

Directions: Use a centimeter ruler to measure each pencil. Subtract to find how many centimeters were lost when sharpening each pencil.

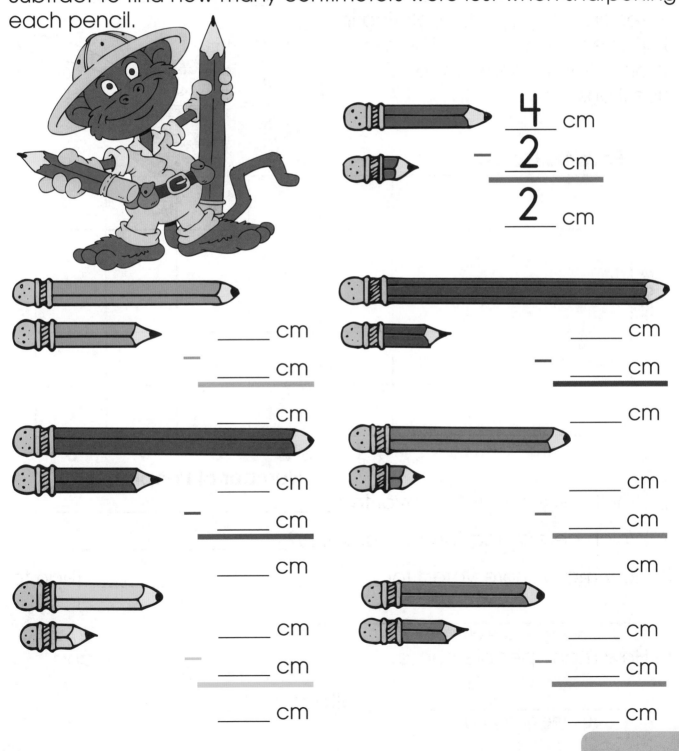

$$\begin{array}{r} \underline{4} \text{ cm} \\ - \underline{2} \text{ cm} \\ \hline \underline{2} \text{ cm} \end{array}$$

_____ cm
_____ cm
_____ cm

_____ cm
− _____ cm
_____ cm

_____ cm
_____ cm
_____ cm

_____ cm
− _____ cm
_____ cm

_____ cm
_____ cm
_____ cm

_____ cm
− _____ cm
_____ cm

Name _____

Good Morning

Directions: Make your own bar graph. List 5 kinds of cereal on the graph below. Ask 5 people to vote for one cereal. Record the votes on the graph by coloring in 1 space for each vote. Use the information to answer the questions.

Favorite Cereal

Cereals

	1	2	3	4	5

Number of People

1. Which cereal was the favorite? _____

2. Which cereal had the fewest votes? _____

3. How many more voted for _____ than for
   (name of cereal)
   _____ ? _____
   (name of cereal)

4. How many people chose _____ and
   (name of cereal)
   _____ altogether? _____
   (name of cereal)

Your Total Solution for Math: Grade 2

Jungle Weather

Directions: The pictures show the weather for one month. Count the number of sunny, cloudy, and rainy days.

Directions: Complete the pictograph using the tallies above.

Weather for 1 Month

Number of Days

Name _____

What a Meal!

Directions: Use the pictograph to complete each sentence below.

= 2 worms

Grace Goldfish	
Willie Walleye	
Calvin Catfish	
Benny Bluegill	
Beth Bass	
Patty Perch	

1. _____ got the fewest worms.

2. _____ got the most worms.

3. _____ and _____ got the same number of worms.

4. Benny and Patty together caught the same number of worms as _____ .

5. Write the number of worms that each fish ate.

_____	_____	_____	_____	_____	_____
Grace	**Willie**	**Calvin**	**Benny**	**Beth**	**Patty**

Your Total Solution for Math: Grade 2

"Play Ball"

Directions: Eight baseball teams have just completed their season. Each team played eight games. Use this pictograph to answer the questions below.

 = I win

Washington Wiggle Worms	⚾ ⚾ ⚾ ⚾ ⚾ ⚾
Jersey Jaguars	⚾ ⚾ ⚾ ⚾ ⚾ ⚾ ⚾
Pittsburgh Pandas	⚾ ⚾ ⚾ ⚾ ⚾
Tampa Toucans	⚾ ⚾ ⚾
Kansas City Centipedes	⚾ ⚾ ⚾ ⚾
Lansing Lightning Bugs	⚾
Houston Hornets	⚾ ⚾
Memphis Monkeys	⚾

1. How many games did the Memphis Monkeys lose? _____

2. Which teams tied for last place?

   _____ and _____

3. Which team won the most games? _____

4. How many more games did the Washington Wiggle Worms win than the Tampa Toucans? _____

5. Which four teams' total number of games won equal the Jersey Jaguars' number of games won? _____

   _____

Name _____

Graphs

A **graph** is a drawing that shows information about numbers.

Directions: Count the apples in each row. Color the boxes to show how many apples have bites taken out of them.

Example:

	1	2	3	4	5	6	7	8

© Carson-Dellosa • CD-704555

Your Total Solution for Math: Grade 2

Graphs

Directions: Count the banana peels in each column. Color the boxes to show how many bananas have been eaten by the monkeys.

Example:

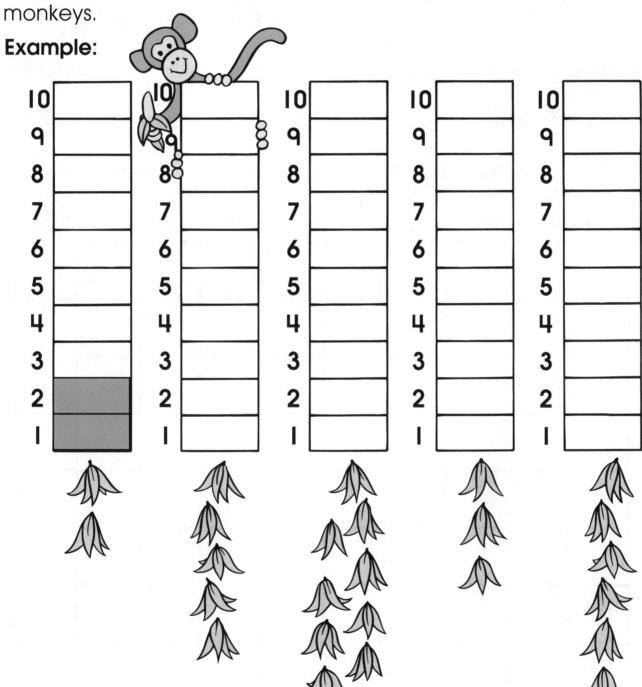

Name _____

Treasure Chest

Directions: Read the directions. Draw the pictures where they belong on the grid. Start at 0 and go . . .

over 2, up 5. Draw a   over 7, up 1. Draw a

over 9, up 3. Draw a    over 6, up 4. Draw a

over 8, up 6. Draw a   over 2, up 3. Draw a

over 5, up 2. Draw a   over 3, up 1. Draw a

over 1, up 7. Draw a   over 4, up 6. Draw a

8										
7										
6										
5										
4										
3										
2										
1										
0	**1**	**2**	**3**	**4**	**5**	**6**	**7**	**8**	**9**	**10**

Your Total Solution for Math: Grade 2

Name _____

Let's Get Things in Order!

Directions: Help Mrs. Brown pick flowers in her garden. The flowers she wants are listed in the chart. Use the descriptions to color the flowers in her garden.

↓	→	Color it:
1st row	6th flower	red
2nd row	4th flower	blue
3rd row	1st flower	yellow
4th row	9th flower	pink
5th row	10th flower	orange
6th row	2nd flower	green
7th row	5th flower	black
8th row	7th flower	grey
9th row	8th flower	purple
10th row	3rd flower	brown

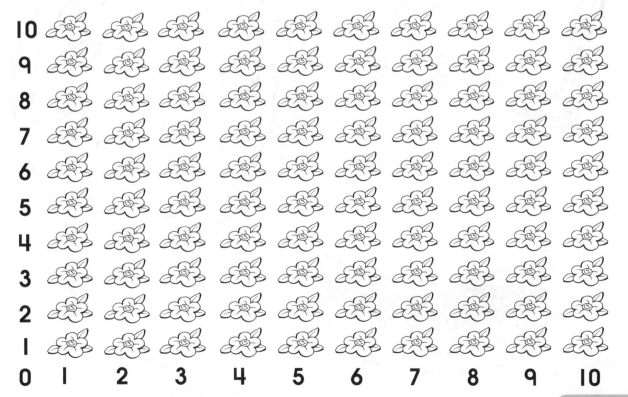

Whole and Half

A **fraction** is a number that names part of a whole, such as $\frac{1}{2}$.

Directions: Color half of each thing.

Example: whole apple   half an apple

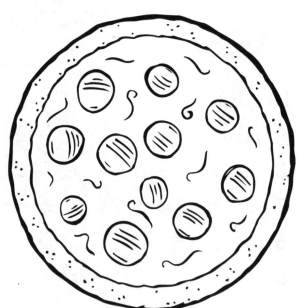

Your Total Solution for Math: Grade 2

Name _____

One Third

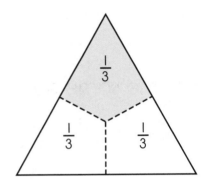

 part is blue.

The ☐ parts are the same size.

$\frac{1}{3}$ of the inside is blue.

Directions: Complete the fraction statements.

Example: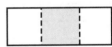

_____ part is blue.
_____ parts are the same size.
_____ of the inside is blue.

_____ part is blue.
_____ parts are the same size.
_____ of the inside is blue.

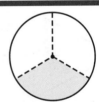

_____ part is blue.
_____ parts are the same size.
_____ of the inside is blue.

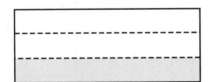

_____ part is blue.
_____ parts are the same size.
_____ of the inside is blue.

_____ of the inside is blue.

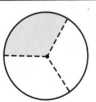

_____ of the inside is blue.

Your Total Solution for Math: Grade 2

© Carson-Dellosa • CD-704555

Name _____

One Fourth

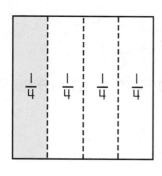

$\dfrac{1}{4}$ $\dfrac{1}{4}$ $\dfrac{1}{4}$ $\dfrac{1}{4}$

 part is blue.

The ⬜ parts are the same size.

$\dfrac{1}{4}$ of the inside is blue.

Directions: Complete the fraction statements.

Example:

_____ part is blue.

_____ parts are the same size.

_____ of the inside is blue.

_____ part is blue.

_____ parts are the same size.

_____ of the inside is blue.

_____ part is blue.

_____ parts are the same size.

_____ of the inside is blue.

_____ part is blue.

_____ parts are the same size.

_____ of the inside is blue.

 _____ of the inside is blue.

 _____ of the inside is blue.

Your Total Solution for Math: Grade 2

Fractions: Half, Third, Fourth

Directions: Study the examples. Circle the fraction that shows the shaded part. Then, circle the fraction that shows the white part.

Examples:

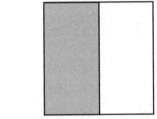 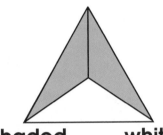 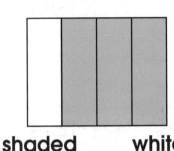

shaded   white   shaded   white   shaded   white

$\frac{1}{4}$ $\frac{1}{3}$ $\left(\frac{1}{2}\right)$ $\frac{1}{3}$ $\left(\frac{1}{2}\right)$ $\frac{1}{4}$ $\frac{1}{2}$ $\left(\frac{2}{3}\right)$ $\frac{3}{4}$ $\frac{2}{3}$ $\frac{1}{2}$ $\left(\frac{1}{3}\right)$ $\frac{1}{4}$ $\frac{1}{2}$ $\left(\frac{3}{4}\right)$ $\left(\frac{1}{4}\right)$ $\frac{2}{3}$ $\frac{1}{2}$

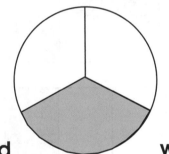   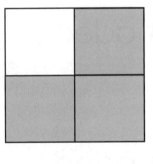

shaded   white   shaded   white

$\frac{1}{4}$ $\frac{1}{3}$ $\frac{1}{2}$ $\frac{2}{4}$ $\frac{2}{3}$ $\frac{2}{2}$ $\frac{3}{4}$ $\frac{1}{3}$ $\frac{3}{2}$ $\frac{1}{2}$ $\frac{1}{4}$ $\frac{1}{3}$

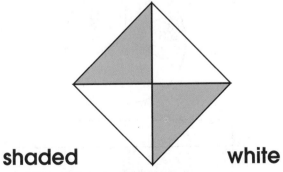   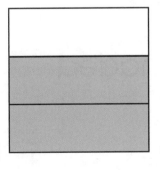

shaded   white   shaded   white

$\frac{2}{3}$ $\frac{2}{4}$ $\frac{2}{2}$ $\frac{1}{3}$ $\frac{2}{4}$ $\frac{2}{2}$ $\frac{1}{3}$ $\frac{2}{3}$ $\frac{2}{2}$ $\frac{1}{2}$ $\frac{1}{4}$ $\frac{1}{3}$

Name _____

Shaded Shapes

Directions: Draw a line to match each fraction with its correct shape.

$\frac{1}{3}$ shaded

$\frac{2}{4}$ shaded

$\frac{1}{4}$ shaded

$\frac{1}{2}$ shaded

$\frac{3}{4}$ shaded

$\frac{2}{3}$ shaded

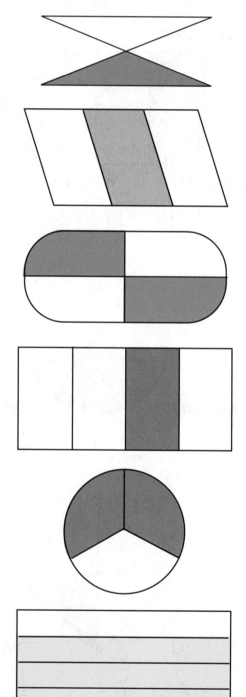

Your Total Solution for Math: Grade 2

Fraction Food

Directions: Count the equal parts. Circle the fraction that names one of the parts.

$\dfrac{1}{2}$ $\dfrac{1}{3}$ $\dfrac{1}{4}$

$\dfrac{1}{2}$ $\dfrac{1}{3}$ $\dfrac{1}{4}$

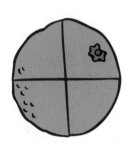

$\dfrac{1}{2}$ $\dfrac{1}{3}$ $\dfrac{1}{4}$

$\dfrac{1}{2}$ $\dfrac{1}{3}$ $\dfrac{1}{4}$

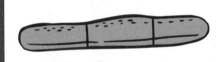

$\dfrac{1}{2}$ $\dfrac{1}{3}$ $\dfrac{1}{4}$

$\dfrac{1}{2}$ $\dfrac{1}{3}$ $\dfrac{1}{4}$

$\dfrac{1}{2}$ $\dfrac{1}{3}$ $\dfrac{1}{4}$

$\dfrac{1}{2}$ $\dfrac{1}{3}$ $\dfrac{1}{4}$

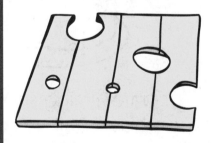

$\dfrac{1}{2}$ $\dfrac{1}{3}$ $\dfrac{1}{4}$

Name _____

Mean Monster's Diet

Directions: Help Mean Monster choose the right piece of food.

1. Mean Monster may have $\frac{1}{4}$ of this chocolate pie. Color in $\frac{1}{4}$ of the pie.

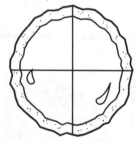

2. For a snack, he wants $\frac{1}{3}$ of this chocolate cake. Color in $\frac{1}{3}$ of the cake.

3. For an evening snack, he can have $\frac{1}{4}$ of the candy bar. Color in $\frac{1}{4}$ of the candy bar.

4. Mean Monster may eat $\frac{1}{3}$ of this pizza. Color in $\frac{1}{3}$ of the pizza.

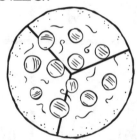

5. For lunch, Mean Monster gets $\frac{1}{2}$ of the sandwich. Color in $\frac{1}{2}$ of the sandwich.

6. He ate $\frac{1}{2}$ of the apple for lunch. Color in $\frac{1}{2}$ of the apple.

Your Total Solution for Math: Grade 2

Fractions

One morning, Mrs. Murky asks her class:

"Which would you rather have, $\frac{1}{2}$ of a candy bar or $\frac{2}{4}$ of a candy bar?"

Directions: Which would you rather have? Explain your answer.

_____

_____

1+2

Name _____

Clocks: Identifying Parts

Directions: A clock face has numbers. Trace the numbers on the clock.

Your Total Solution for Math: Grade 2

Writing the Time

Directions: Color the little hour hand **red**. Fill in the blanks.

The **BIG HAND** is on _____ .

The **little hand** is on _____ .

It is _____ o'clock.

The **BIG HAND** is on _____ .

The **little hand** is on _____ .

It is _____ o'clock.

The **BIG HAND** is on _____ .

The **little hand** is on _____ .

It is _____ o'clock.

The **BIG HAND** is on _____ .

The **little hand** is on _____ .

It is _____ o'clock.

Name _____

Practice

Directions: What is the time?

_____ o'clock

_____ o'clock

_____ o'clock

_____ o'clock

_____ o'clock

_____ o'clock

_____ o'clock

_____ o'clock

_____ o'clock

_____ o'clock

_____ o'clock

_____ o'clock

Your Total Solution for Math: Grade 2

Matching Digital and Face Clocks

Long ago, there were only wind-up clocks. Today, we also have electric and battery clocks. We may soon have solar clocks!

Directions: Match the digital and face clocks that show the same time.

Name _____

Writing Time on the Half-Hour

Directions: Write the times.

_____

_____ minutes past

_____

_____ minutes past

_____

_____ o'clock

_____

_____ o'clock

What is your dinner time?

Directions: Circle the time you eat.

Your Total Solution for Math: Grade 2

Name _____

Writing Time on the Half-Hour

Directions: What time is it?

_____

_____

_____

_____

_____

_____

Time to the Quarter-Hour: Introduction

Each **hour** has **60** minutes. An **hour** has **4 quarter-hours**. A **quarter-hour** is **15 minutes**.

This clock face shows a quarter of an hour.

From the **12** to the **3** is **15 minutes**.

From the 12 to the 3 is 15 minutes.

_____15_____ minutes after _____8_____ o'clock

is _____8:15_____.

Your Total Solution for Math: Grade 2

Writing Time on the Quarter-Hour

Directions: Draw the hands. Write the times.

5:15

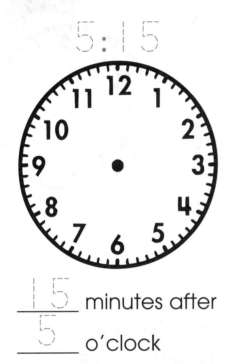

__15__ minutes after

__5__ o'clock

10:15

_____ minutes after

_____ o'clock

2:15

_____ minutes after

_____ o'clock

9:15

_____ minutes after

_____ o'clock

Name _____

Time to the Minute Intervals: Introduction

Each **number** on the clock face stands for **5** minutes.

Directions: Count by **5**s beginning at the **12**.
Write the numbers here:

 00   05   10   15   20   25
___ ___ ___ ___ ___ ___

It is __25__ minutes after __8__ o'clock. It is written 8:25.

Directions: Count by **5**s.

 00
___ ___ ___ ___ ___ ___ ___ ___

It is _____ minutes after _____ o'clock.

_____ : _____

Your Total Solution for Math: Grade 2

Drawing the Minute Hand

Directions: Draw the hands on these fish clocks.

7:45   8:05   11:15

3:20   5:55   1:50

12:10   10:25   4:40

Name _____

Counting Pennies

Directions: Count the pennies. How many cents?

Example:

    = **4¢**

         = ☐

     = ☐

          = ☐

   = ☐

   = ☐

      = ☐

  = ☐

         = ☐

Your Total Solution for Math: Grade 2

Counting Pennies

Directions: Count the pennies in each triangle.

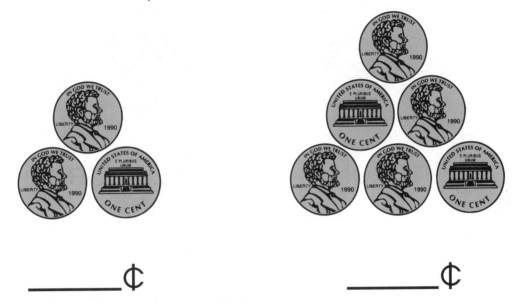

_____¢   _____¢

_____¢

Name _____

Nickels: Introduction

Directions: Look at the two sides of a nickel. Color the nickels **silver**.

front   back

_____1_____ nickel   =   _____5_____ pennies

_____1_____ nickel   =   _____5_____ cents

_____1_____ nickel   =   _____5_____ ¢

Directions: Write the number of cents in a nickel.

5¢ = ____¢ + ____¢ + ____¢ + ____¢ + ____¢

=

Your Total Solution for Math: Grade 2

Name _____

Nickels: Counting by Fives

Directions: Count the nickels by 5s. Write the amount.

Example:

5 cents = 1 nickel

    15 ¢   ☐ ¢

Count __5__, __10__, __15__.   Count ____, ____.

     ☐ ¢   ☐ ¢

Count ____, ____, ____,   Count ____, ____, ____, ____

____, ____.   ____, ____.

     ☐ ¢   ☐ ¢

Count ____, ____, ____,   Count ____, ____, ____,

____.   ____, ____, ____.

Dimes: Introduction

A dime is small, but quite strong. It can buy more than a penny or a nickel.

front   back

Directions: Each side of a dime is different. It has ridges on its edge. Color the dime **silver**.

Directions: Write the number of cents in a dime.

_____ dime   =   _____ pennies

_____ dime   =   _____ cents

_____ dime   =   _____ ¢

Your Total Solution for Math: Grade 2

Dimes: Counting by Tens

Directions: Count by 10s. Write the number. Circle the group with more.

_____ ¢   or   _____ ¢

_____ ¢   or   _____ ¢

_____ ¢   or   _____ ¢

Quarters: Introduction

Our first president, George Washington, is on the front. The American eagle is on the back.

front   back

Directions: Write the number of cents in a quarter.

_____ quarter = _____ pennies

_____ quarter = _____ cents

_____ quarter = _____ ¢

Directions: Count these nickels by 5s. Is this another way to make 25 ¢ ?

yes   no

Your Total Solution for Math: Grade 2

Counting with Quarters

These are some machines that use quarters.

Directions: Color each machine you have to put quarters into. Circle the number of quarters you need.

I need _____ quarters to wash clothes.

I need _____ quarter(s) to make a phone call.

Name _____

Counting with Quarters, Dimes, Nickels, and Pennies

Directions: Match the money with the amount.

35 ¢

36 ¢

40 ¢

27 ¢

15 ¢

21 ¢

8 ¢

Your Total Solution for Math: Grade 2

Counting with Quarters, Dimes, Nickels, and Pennies

Here are things to buy for your hair.

Directions: How many of each coin do you need?
Write 1, 2, 3, or 4.

	Quarters	Dimes	Nickels	Pennies
(flower)				
(brush)				
(band)				
(bow)				
(comb)				

Subtracting for Change

Adam wanted to know how much change he would have left when he bought things. He made this picture to help him subtract.

$$
\begin{array}{r}
4 \text{ dimes} \\
- 1 \text{ dime} \\
\hline
3 \text{ dimes}
\end{array}
\qquad
\begin{array}{r}
40 \text{ ¢} \\
-10 \text{ ¢} \\
\hline
30 \text{ ¢}
\end{array}
$$

Directions: Cross out and subtract.

$$
\begin{array}{r}
6 \text{ dimes} \\
- 4 \text{ dimes} \\
\hline
 \text{ dimes}
\end{array}
\qquad
\begin{array}{r}
60 \text{ ¢} \\
-40 \text{ ¢} \\
\hline
 \text{ ¢}
\end{array}
$$

Your Total Solution for Math: Grade 2

Name _____

Problem-Solving with Money

Directions: Draw the coins you use. Write the number of coins on each blank.

1.

9¢

_____ dimes

_____ nickels

_____ pennies

2.

11¢

_____ dimes

_____ nickels

_____ pennies

3.

14¢

_____ dimes

_____ nickels

_____ pennies

4. Find another way to pay for the

14¢

_____ dimes

_____ nickels

_____ pennies

Name _____

Making Exact Amounts of Money: Two Ways to Pay

Directions: Find two ways to pay. Show what coins you use.

1.

_____ quarters

_____ dimes

_____ nickels

_____ pennies

2.

_____ quarters

_____ dimes

_____ nickels

_____ pennies

3.

_____ quarters

_____ dimes

_____ nickels

_____ pennies

4.

_____ quarters

_____ dimes

_____ nickels

_____ pennies

Your Total Solution for Math: Grade 2

Making Exact Amounts of Money: How Much More?

Directions: Count the coins. Find out how much more money you need to pay the exact amount.

How much money do you have? _____ ¢

How much more money do you need? _____ ¢

How much money do you have? _____ ¢

How much more money do you need? _____ ¢

Solve this puzzle.

How much more money does Monkey need?

_____ ¢

I have 1 quarter and 4 dimes. I need one more coin to pay for the banana-van.

75¢

How to Help Your Child Prepare for Standardized Testing

Preparing All Year Round
Perhaps the most valuable way you can help your child prepare for standardized achievement tests is by providing enriching experiences. Keep in mind also that test results for younger children are not as reliable as for older students. If a child is hungry, tired, or upset, this may result in a poor test score. Here are some tips on how you can help your child do his or her best on standardized tests.

Read aloud with your child. Reading aloud helps develop vocabulary and fosters a positive attitude toward reading. Reading together is one of the most effective ways you can help your child succeed in school.

Share experiences. Baking cookies together, planting a garden, or making a map of your neighborhood are examples of activities that help build skills that are measured on the tests, such as sequencing and following directions.

Become informed about your state's testing procedures. Ask about or watch for announcements of meetings that explain about standardized tests and statewide assessments in your school district. Talk to your child's teacher about your child's individual performance on these state tests during a parent-teacher conference.

Help your child know what to expect. Read and discuss with your child the test-taking tips in this book. Your child can prepare by working through a couple of strategies a day so that no practice session takes too long.

Help your child with his or her regular school assignments. Set up a quiet study area for homework. Supply this area with pencils, paper, markers, a calculator, a ruler, a dictionary, scissors, glue, and so on. Check your child's homework and offer to help if he or she gets stuck. But remember, it's your child's homework, not yours. If you help too much, your child will not benefit from the activity.

Keep in regular contact with your child's teacher. Attend parent-teacher conferences, school functions, PTA or PTO meetings, and school board meetings. This will help you get to know the educators in your district and the families of your child's classmates.

Learn to use computers as an educational resource. If you do not have a computer and Internet access at home, try your local library.

Remember—simply getting your child comfortable with testing procedures and helping him or her know what to expect can improve test scores!

Getting Ready for the Big Day

There are lots of things you can do on or immediately before test day to improve your child's chances of testing success. What's more, these strategies will help your child prepare him- or herself for school tests, too, and promote general study skills that can last a lifetime.

Provide a good breakfast on test day. Instead of sugar cereal, which provides immediate but not long-term energy, have your child eat a breakfast with protein or complex carbohydrates, such as an egg, whole grain cereal or toast, or a banana-yogurt shake.

Promote a good night's sleep. A good night's sleep before the test is essential. Try not to overstress the importance of the test. This may cause your child to lose sleep because of anxiety. Doing some exercise after school and having a quiet evening routine will help your child sleep well the night before the test.

Assure your child that he or she is not expected to know all of the answers on the test. Explain that other children in higher grades may take the same test, and that the test may measure things your child has not yet learned in school. Help your child understand that you expect him or her to put forth a good effort—and that this is enough. Your child should not try to cram for these tests. Also avoid threats or bribes; these put undue pressure on children and may interfere with their best performance.

Keep the mood light and offer encouragement. To provide a break on test days, do something fun and special after school—take a walk around the neighborhood, play a game, read a favorite book, or prepare a special snack together. These activities keep your child's mood light—even if the testing sessions have been difficult—and show how much you appreciate your child's effort.

Name _____

Mathematics Practice Test

Lesson 1 Mathematics Skills

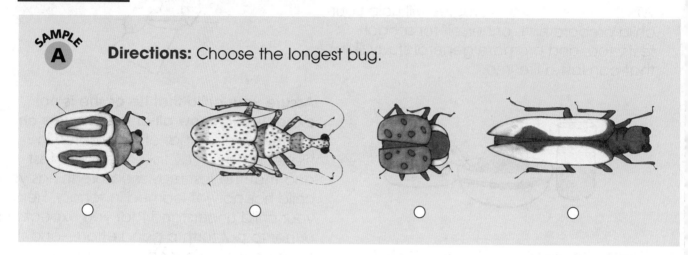

SAMPLE A **Directions:** Choose the longest bug.

Listen carefully while you look at the problem and all the answer choices.

Listen for key words and numbers.

Mark the right answer as soon as you know which one it is. Then get ready for the next item.

GO

Your Total Solution for Math: Grade 2

Mathematics Practice Test

1 What number is shown on the place value chart?

36	360	306	63
○	○	○	○

---

2 Find the shape that is one-third shaded.

Shape 1	Shape 2	Shape 3	Shape 4
○	○	○	○

---

3 Which number sentence can be used to show the total number of books?

○ $4 + 2 = \square$ ○ $2 + 2 + 2 + 2 = \square$

○ $4 + 4 + 4 + 4 = \square$ ○ $4 + 4 = \square$

GO

1+2

Name _____

Mathematics Practice Test

4   Which tool would students use to measure a pint of water from the stream?

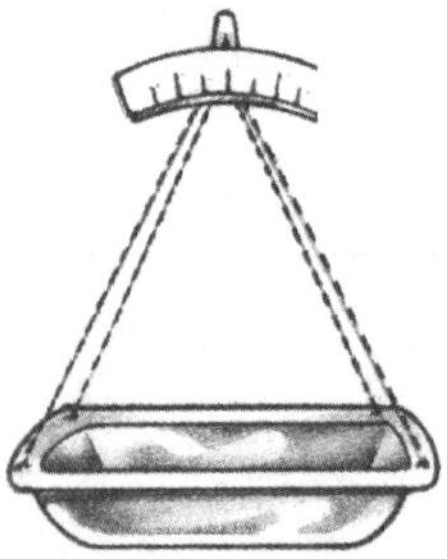

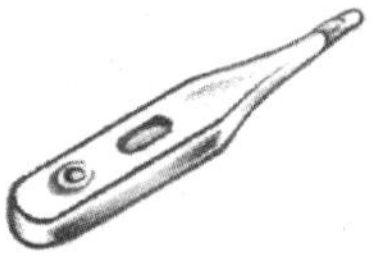

hanging scale   tape measure   measuring cup   thermometer
   ○   ○   ○   ○

---

5   Pablo has two quarters, one dime, and three nickels. How much money does he have in all?

   75¢   65¢   60¢   70¢
    ○   ○   ○   ○

GO

Your Total Solution for Math: Grade 2

Mathematics Practice Test

6 Which child is third from the lifeguard?

Ann ○   Tom ○   Reg ○   Beth ○

---

7 Which squares contain numbers that are all less than 19?

○ 7 15 10 18   ○ 18 6 23 65

○ 91 20 32 57   ○ 12 81 17 44

---

8 Which answer choice names a shape not in the circle?

○ cone   ○ box

○ can   ○ ball

---

9 Which number is missing from the pattern?

3 5 7   11 13

6 ○   8 ○   9 ○   10 ○   GO

Mathematics Practice Test

Directions: The students in Mr. Naldo's class are having a Math Fair. One of the games is a number wheel. The chart shows how many times the spinner landed on each number after 20 spins. Use the chart to do numbers 10 and 11.

Number	1	2	3
Spins	ＵＨＩ	ＩＩＩ	ＵＨＩ ＵＨＩ ＩＩ

10 How many times did the spinner land on the number 3?

    3 ○   5 ○   7 ○   12 ○

11 Which spinner looks most like the one the students are using?

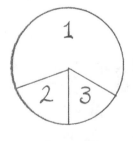   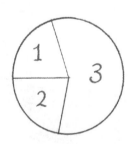   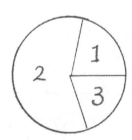   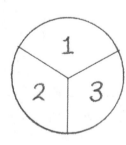

   spinner 1   spinner 2   spinner 3   spinner 4

    ○   ○   ○   ○

STOP

         Your Total Solution for Math: Grade 2

Name _____

Mathematics Practice Test

Lesson 2 Review

SAMPLE A **Directions:** A train left the station at 9:30. It arrived in Sharon Hill twenty minutes later. Which clock shows the time the train arrived?

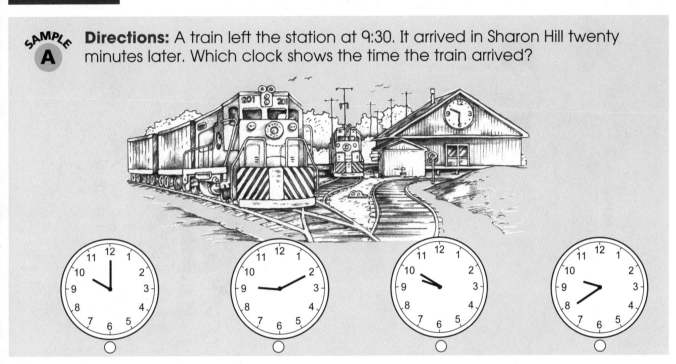

1   Four planes are on the ground at the airport. Two more planes land. How many planes are on the ground all together?

○ 8

○ 6

○ 7

○ 2

2   Find the calendar that has thirty-one days.

June ○   September ○   October ○   November ○   GO

Name _____

Mathematics Practice Test

Directions: The bar graph shows how many fish are in a pond at a school's nature center. Use the graph to do numbers 3–5 on the next page.

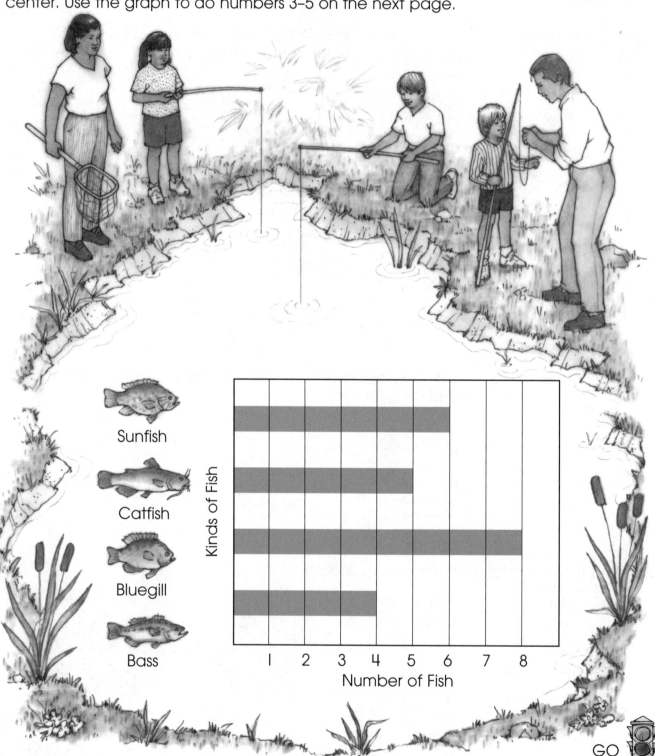

Sunfish

Catfish

Bluegill

Bass

Kinds of Fish

Number of Fish

GO

Your Total Solution for Math: Grade 2

Mathematics Practice Test

3 Look at the graph. What kind of fish are there fewest of in the pond?

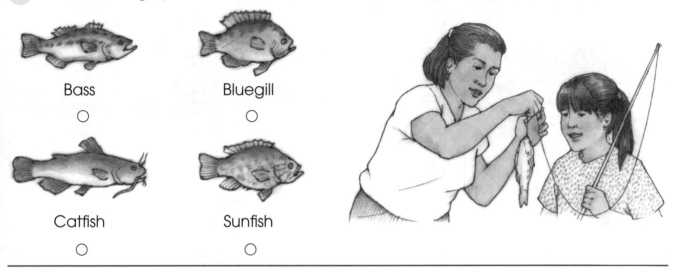

Bass
○

Bluegill
○

Catfish
○

Sunfish
○

4 The average weight of the sunfish in the pond is six ounces. How much do the sunfish in the pond weigh all together? One pound equals 16 ounces.

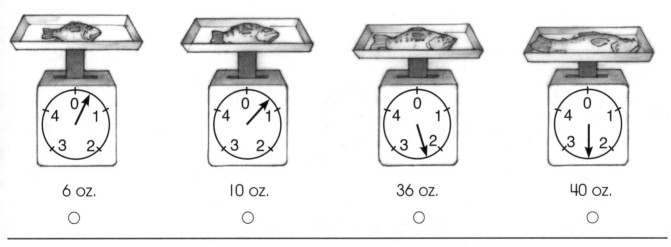

6 oz.
○

10 oz.
○

36 oz.
○

40 oz.
○

5 Nadia counted eight of this kind of fish in the pond. What kind of fish did she count?

Bass
○

Bluegill
○

Catfish
○

Sunfish
○

STOP

Answer Key

Dapper Dog's Campout

Directions: Dapper Dog is going on a camping trip. Draw an **X** on the word in each row that does not belong.

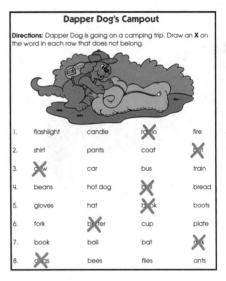

1.	flashlight	candle	~~radio~~	fire
2.	shirt	pants	coat	~~bat~~
3.	~~cow~~	car	bus	train
4.	beans	hot dog	~~ball~~	bread
5.	gloves	hat	~~book~~	boots
6.	fork	~~butter~~	cup	plate
7.	book	ball	bat	~~milk~~
8.	~~dogs~~	bees	flies	ants

4

Classification Fun

Directions: Write each word in the correct row at the bottom of the page.

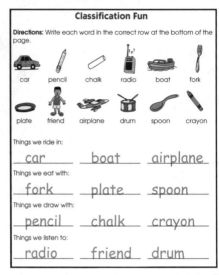

car   pencil   chalk   radio   boat   fork
plate   friend   airplane   drum   spoon   crayon

Things we ride in:
car   boat   airplane

Things we eat with:
fork   plate   spoon

Things we draw with:
pencil   chalk   crayon

Things we listen to:
radio   friend   drum

5

Where Does It Belong?

Directions: Read the words in the fish tank. Write each word in its correct place.

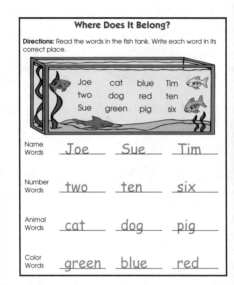

Joe   cat   blue   Tim
two   dog   red   ten
Sue   green   pig   six

Name Words	Joe	Sue	Tim
Number Words	two	ten	six
Animal Words	cat	dog	pig
Color Words	green	blue	red

6

Classifying

Directions: The words in each list form a group. Choose the word from the box that describes each group and write it on the line.

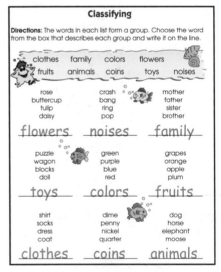

clothes   family   colors   flowers
fruits   animals   coins   toys   noises

rose buttercup tulip daisy	crash bang ring pop	mother father sister brother
flowers	noises	family
puzzle wagon blocks doll	green purple blue red	grapes orange apple plum
toys	colors	fruits
shirt socks dress coat	dime penny nickel quarter	dog horse elephant moose
clothes	coins	animals

7

Classifying: Foods

Darcy likes fruit and things made from fruit. She also likes bread.

Directions: Circle the things on the menu that Darcy will eat.

MENU

(apple pie)	corn
peas	(rolls)
beans	(banana bread)
(oranges)	(grape drink)
chicken	

8

Classifying: Animal Habitats

Directions: Read the story. Then, write each animal's name under **WATER** or **LAND** to tell where it lives.

Animals live in different habitats. A **habitat** is the place of an animal's natural home. Many animals live on land and others live in water. Most animals that live in water breathe with gills. Animals that live on land breathe with lungs.

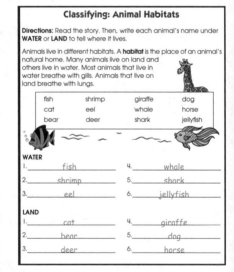

fish	shrimp	giraffe	dog
cat	eel	whale	horse
bear	deer	shark	jellyfish

WATER

1. fish	4. whale
2. shrimp	5. shark
3. eel	6. jellyfish

LAND

1. cat	4. giraffe
2. bear	5. dog
3. deer	6. horse

9

Your Total Solution for Math: Grade 2

Answer Key

Happy Hikers

Directions: Trace a path through the maze by counting from 1 to 10 in the correct order. Color the picture.

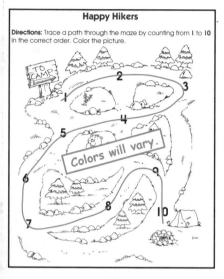

Colors will vary.

10

Zany Zoo

Directions: Count and color each group of animals. Cut out the numbers and glue them in the correct boxes.

Colors will vary.

11

Rainbow-Colored Numbers

Directions: Color the spaces: 1 = red, 2 = blue, 3 = yellow, 4 = green, and 5 = orange

13

Clown Capers

Directions: Count the number of each thing in the picture. Write the number on the line.

14

Take an Animal Count!

Directions: Count each group of zoo animals. Draw a line from the number to the correct number word. The first one shows you what to do.

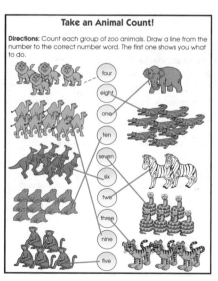

15

Number Words

Directions: Number the buildings from one to six.

Directions: Draw a line from the word to the number.

two — 1
five — 3
six — 5
four — 6
one — 2
three — 4

16

ANSWER KEY

Answer Key

Number Words

Directions: Number the buildings from five to ten.

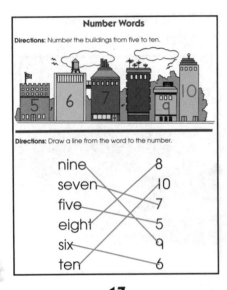

5   6   7   10   9

Directions: Draw a line from the word to the number.

nine ─── 8
seven ─── 10
five ─── 7
eight ─── 5
six ─── 9
ten ─── 6

17

Sequencing Numbers

Sequencing is putting numbers in the correct order.

Directions: Write the missing numbers.

Example: 4, _5_, 6

3, _4_, 5   7, _8_, 9   8, _9_, 10

6, _7_, 8   _2_, 3, 4   _4_, 5, 6

5, 6, _7_   _5_, 6, 7   _2_, 3, 4

_8_, 9, 10   _6_, 7, 8   2, _3_, 4

2, 3, _4_   1, 2, _3_   7, 8, _9_

2, _3_, 4   _6_, 7, 8   4, _5_, 6

6, 7, _8_   2, 3, _4_   1, _2_, 3

7, 8, _9_   _2_, 3, 4   _8_, 9, 10

18

Counting

Directions: Write the numbers that are:

next in order	one less	one greater
22, 23, _24_, _25_	_15_, 16	6, _7_
674, _675_, _676_	_246_, 247	125, _126_
227, _228_, _229_	_549_, 550	499, _500_
199, _200_, _201_	_332_, 333	750, _751_
329, _330_, _331_	_861_, 862	933, _934_

Directions: Write the missing numbers.

13 14 15 16 17 18

163 164 165 166 167 168

821 822 823 824 825 826

19

Note the Count

Directions: Count the number of notes on each page of music. Write the number on the line below it. In each box, circle the greater number of notes.

8   6   4   7

10   9   8   9

Directions: Color the note in each box that is greater.

49 25   19 41

32 54   38 29   35 46   37 43

20

Teddy Bears in a Row

Directions: Cut out the bears at the bottom of the page. Glue them where they belong in number order.

39 40 41   29 30 31
10 11 12   78 79 80
84 85 86   64 65 66

21

Plump Piglets

Directions: Read the clues to find out how many ears of corn each pig ate. Write the number on the line below each pig.

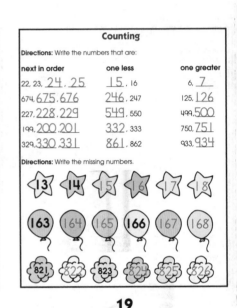

I ate the number that comes before **26**.   Patsy 25

I ate the number that comes between **87** and **89**.   Horace 88

I ate the number that comes after **92**.   Pinky 93

I ate the number that comes before **57**.   Hilda 56

I ate the number that comes between **39** and **41**.   Porky 40

Who ate the most? _Pinky_   Who ate the least? _Patsy_

23

Your Total Solution for Math: Grade 2

Answer Key

Counting by Twos

Directions: Count by **2**s to draw the path to the store.

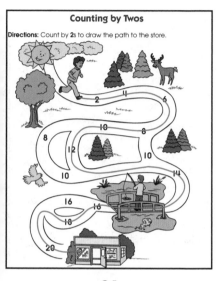

24

Two for the Pool

Directions: Count by **2**s. Write the numbers to **30** in the water drops. Begin at the top of the slide and go down.

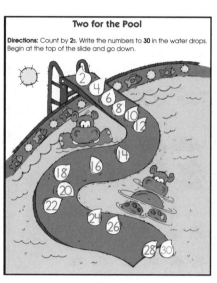

25

Counting by Fives

Directions: Count by **5**s to draw the path to the playground.

26

Cookie Clues

Directions: Find out what holds something good! Count by **5**s to connect the dots. Color the picture.

Colors will vary.

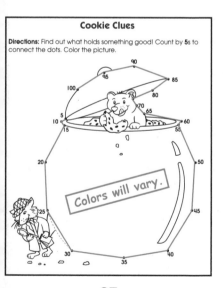

27

Desert Trek

Directions: Count by **10**s. Color each canteen with a **10** to lead the camel to the watering hole.

28

Caterpillar Count

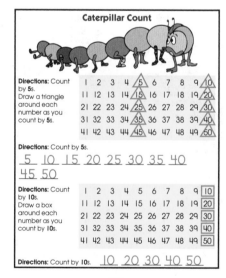

Directions: Count by **5**s. Draw a triangle around each number as you count by **5**s.

1	2	3	4	5△	6	7	8	9	10△
11	12	13	14	15△	16	17	18	19	20△
21	22	23	24	25△	26	27	28	29	30△
31	32	33	34	35△	36	37	38	39	40△
41	42	43	44	45△	46	47	48	49	50△

Directions: Count by **5**s.

_5_ _10_ _15_ _20_ _25_ _30_ _35_ _40_
_45_ _50_

Directions: Count by **10**s. Draw a box around each number as you count by **10**s.

1	2	3	4	5	6	7	8	9	10☐
11	12	13	14	15	16	17	18	19	20☐
21	22	23	24	25	26	27	28	29	30☐
31	32	33	34	35	36	37	38	39	40☐
41	42	43	44	45	46	47	48	49	50☐

Directions: Count by **10**s. _10_ _20_ _30_ _40_ _50_

29

Answer Key

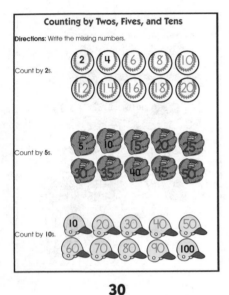

Counting by Twos, Fives, and Tens

Directions: Write the missing numbers.

Count by 2s.
2 4 6 8 10
12 14 16 18 20

Count by 5s.
5 10 15 20 25
30 35 40 45 50

Count by 10s.
10 20 30 40 50
60 70 80 90 100

30

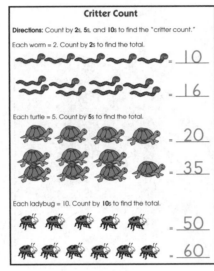

Critter Count

Directions: Count by 2s, 5s, and 10s to find the "critter count."

Each worm = 2. Count by 2s to find the total.
= 10
= 16

Each turtle = 5. Count by 5s to find the total.
= 20
= 35

Each ladybug = 10. Count by 10s to find the total.
= 50
= 60

31

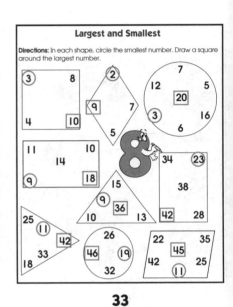

Largest and Smallest

Directions: In each shape, circle the smallest number. Draw a square around the largest number.

33

Less Than, Greater Than

Directions: The open mouth points to the larger number. The small point goes to the smaller number. Draw the symbol < or > to the correct number.

Example: 5 (>) 3 — This means that 5 is greater than 3, and 3 is less than 5.

12 (>) 2   16 (>) 6

16 (>) 15   1 (<) 2

7 (>) 1   19 (>) 5

9 (>) 6   11 (<) 13

34

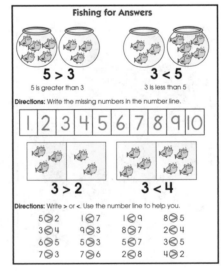

Fishing for Answers

5 > 3   **3 < 5**
5 is greater than 3   3 is less than 5

Directions: Write the missing numbers in the number line.

| 1 | 2 | 3 | 4 | 5 | 6 | 7 | 8 | 9 | 10 |

3 > 2   **3 < 4**

Directions: Write > or <. Use the number line to help you.

5 > 2   1 < 7   1 < 9   8 > 5
3 < 4   9 > 3   8 > 7   2 < 4
6 > 5   5 > 3   5 < 7   3 > 5
7 > 3   7 > 6   2 < 8   4 > 2

35

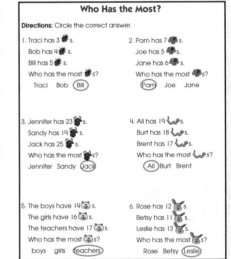

Who Has the Most?

Directions: Circle the correct answer.

1. Traci has 3 s.
   Bob has 4 s.
   Bill has 5 s.
   Who has the most s?
   Traci   Bob   (Bill)

2. Pam has 7 s.
   Joe has 5 s.
   Jane has 6 s.
   Who has the most s?
   (Pam)   Joe   Jane

3. Jennifer has 23 s.
   Sandy has 19 s.
   Jack has 25 s.
   Who has the most s?
   Jennifer   Sandy   (Jack)

4. Ali has 19 s.
   Burt has 18 s.
   Brent has 17 s.
   Who has the most s?
   (Ali)   Burt   Brent

5. The boys have 14 s.
   The girls have 16 s.
   The teachers have 17 s.
   Who has the most s?
   boys   girls   (teachers)

6. Rose has 12 s.
   Betsy has 11 s.
   Leslie has 13 s.
   Who has the most s?
   Rose   Betsy   (Leslie)

36

Your Total Solution for Math: Grade 2

Answer Key

Who Has the Fewest?

Directions: Circle the correct answer.

1. Pat had 4 📷 s.
   Charles had 3 📷 s.
   Andrea had 5 📷 s.
   Who had the fewest number of 📷 s?
   Pat (Charles) Andrea

2. Jeff has 5 🎈 s.
   John has 4 🎈 s.
   Bill has 6 🎈 s.
   Who has the fewest number of 🎈 s?
   Jeff (John) Bill

3. Jane has 7 ⚪ s.
   Susan has 9 ⚪ s.
   Fred has 8 ⚪ s.
   Who has the fewest number of ⚪ s?
   (Jane) Susan Fred

4. Charles bought 12 ⚪ s.
   Rose bought 6 ⚪ s.
   Dawn bought 24 ⚪ s.
   Who bought the fewest number of ⚪ s?
   Charles (Rose) Dawn

5. John had 9 ⚫ s.
   Jack had 8 ⚫ s.
   Mark had 7 ⚫ s.
   Who had the fewest number of ⚫ s?
   John Jack (Mark)

6. Edith bought 12 ⬡ s.
   Michelle bought 16 ⬡ s.
   Marty bought 13 ⬡ s.
   Who bought the fewest number of ⬡ s?
   (Edith) Michelle Marty

37

Orderly Ordinals

Directions: Write each word on the correct line to put the words in order.

second	fifth	seventh	first	tenth
third	eighth	sixth	fourth	ninth

1. first
2. second
3. third
4. fourth
5. fifth
6. sixth
7. seventh
8. eighth
9. ninth
10. tenth

Directions: Which picture is circled in each row? Underline the word that tells the correct number.

third <u>fourth</u>

fourth sixth

first <u>ninth</u>

<u>third</u> fifth

fifth sixth

<u>second</u> third

38

Which Place in the Race?

Directions: Write the correct word to tell each runner's place in the race.

fifth
first
fourth
third
seventh
second
sixth

39

Flags First

Directions:
Color the ninth flag red.
Write **O** on the second flag.
Color the eighth flag blue.
Write **D** on the first flag.
Color the sixth flag yellow.
Write **G** on the fourth flag.
Color the tenth flag purple.
Write **O** on the third flag.
Color the seventh flag green.
Color the fifth flag orange.
What word did you spell? __Good__

40

Swimming in Style!

Directions: Color the swimsuits. The first person is wearing a yellow mask.

Color the fourth suit brown.
Color the second suit purple.
Color the first suit red.
Color the seventh suit pink.
Color the third suit blue.
Color the eighth suit green.
Color the fifth suit orange.
Color the sixth suit yellow.

41

How Many Robots in All?

Directions: Look at the pictures. Complete the addition sentences.

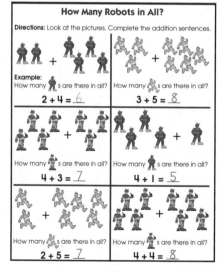

Example:
How many 🤖 s are there in all?
$2 + 4 = 6$

How many 🤖 s are there in all?
$3 + 5 = 8$

How many 🤖 s are there in all?
$4 + 3 = 7$

How many 🤖 s are there in all?
$4 + 1 = 5$

How many 🤖 s are there in all?
$2 + 5 = 7$

How many 🤖 s are there in all?
$4 + 4 = 8$

42

Answer Key

How Many Rabbits?

Directions: Look at the pictures. Complete the addition sentences.

Example:
How many 🐰s are there in all?
$1 + 1 = 2$

How many 🐰s are there in all?
$3 + 6 = 9$

How many 🐰s are there in all?
$6 + 1 = 7$

How many 🐰s are there in all?
$3 + 4 = 7$

How many 🐰s are there in all?
$4 + 5 = 9$

How many 🐰s are there in all?
$2 + 3 = 5$

43

Signs of Gain

Directions: Roll a die. Write the addend from the die in the top box. Add to find the sum. Roll again to make each sentence different.

Answers will vary.

44

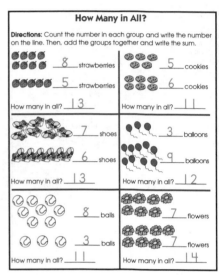

How Many in All?

Directions: Count the number in each group and write the number on the line. Then, add the groups together and write the sum.

8 strawberries
5 strawberries
How many in all? 13

5 cookies
6 cookies
How many in all? 11

7 shoes
6 shoes
How many in all? 13

3 balloons
9 balloons
How many in all? 12

8 balls
3 balls
How many in all? 11

7 flowers
7 flowers
How many in all? 14

45

Adding 1

Directions: Write a number in the top box of each problem. Complete the problem. Make each problem different.

10   14

+ 1   + 1

11

Answers will vary.

46

Counting Up

Directions: Count up to get the sum. Write the missing addend in each blank.

$3 + 3 = 6$
$4 + 1 = 5$
$7 + 2 = 9$
$2 + 2 = 4$
$3 + 5 = 8$
$5 + 0 = 5$
$8 + 2 = 10$
$7 + 1 = 8$
$6 + 3 = 9$

$8 + 1 = 9$
$4 + 2 = 6$
$6 + 0 = 6$
$5 + 2 = 7$
$4 + 3 = 7$
$9 + 1 = 10$
$5 + 3 = 8$
$7 + 3 = 10$
$6 + 2 = 8$

47

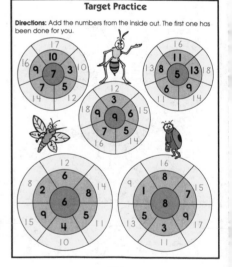

Target Practice

Directions: Add the numbers from the inside out. The first one has been done for you.

48

Your Total Solution for Math: Grade 2

1+2

Answer Key

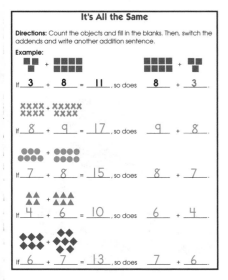

It's All the Same

Directions: Count the objects and fill in the blanks. Then, switch the addends and write another addition sentence.

Example:

If __3__ + __8__ = __11__, so does __8__ + __3__.

If __8__ + __9__ = __17__, so does __9__ + __8__.

If __7__ + __8__ = __15__, so does __8__ + __7__.

If __4__ + __6__ = __10__, so does __6__ + __4__.

If __6__ + __7__ = __13__, so does __7__ + __6__.

49

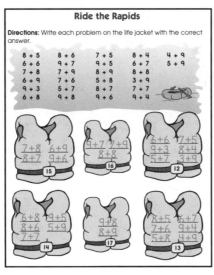

Ride the Rapids

Directions: Write each problem on the life jacket with the correct answer.

8 + 5	8 + 6	7 + 5	8 + 4	4 + 9
6 + 6	9 + 7	9 + 5	6 + 7	5 + 9
7 + 8	8 + 9	8 + 8		
6 + 9	7 + 8	5 + 8	3 + 9	
9 + 3	5 + 7	8 + 7	7 + 7	
6 + 8	9 + 8	9 + 6	9 + 4	

50

Math-Minded Mermaids

Directions: Look at each number. Then, look in each seashell. Circle each pair of numbers that can be added together to equal that number.

51

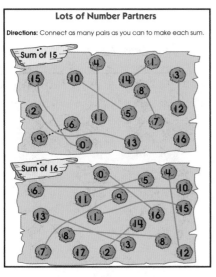

Lots of Number Partners

Directions: Connect as many pairs as you can to make each sum.

Sum of 15

Sum of 16

52

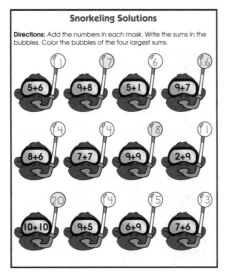

Snorkeling Solutions

Directions: Add the numbers in each mask. Write the sums in the bubbles. Color the bubbles of the four largest sums.

53

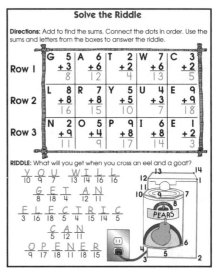

Solve the Riddle

Directions: Add to find the sums. Connect the dots in order. Use the sums and letters from the boxes to answer the riddle.

Row 1	G 5 +3 8	A 6 +6 12	T 2 +2 4	W 7 +6 13	C 3 +2 5
Row 2	L 8 +8 16	R 7 +8 15	Y 5 +5 10	U 4 +3 7	E 9 +9 18
Row 3	N 2 +9 11	O 5 +4 9	P 9 +8 17	I 6 +8 14	E 1 +2 3

RIDDLE: What will you get when you cross an eel and a goat?

Y O U   W I L L
10 7   13 14 11 16

G E T   A N
13 18   4 12 11

E L E C T R I C
3 16 18 5 4 15 14 5

C A N
5 12 11

O P E N E R
9 17 18 11 18 15

54

Answer Key

Coloring by Number

Directions: Find each sum.
If the sum is 13, color the space **brown**.
If the sum is 14, color the space yellow.
If the sum is 16, color the space **red**.
If the sum is 17, color the space **blue**.

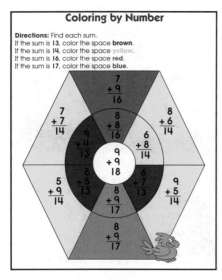

55

Counting Up the Coins

Directions: Solve the problem on each bag. Write the answer on the coin below it. Color the odd sums yellow.

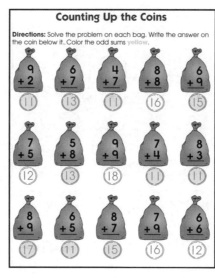

56

Mys-sss-terious Music

Directions: Solve the problems. Color the spaces using the answers.

ANSWER COLOR KEY:

= 0 – 2
= 3 – 6
= 7 – 9
= 10 – 12
= 13 – 16
= 17 – 20

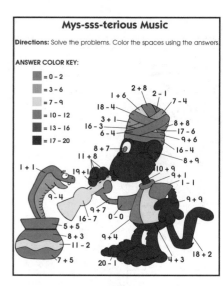

57

Problem Solving

Directions: Solve each problem.

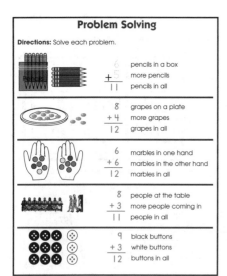

58

Problem Solving

Directions: Solve each problem.
Example:

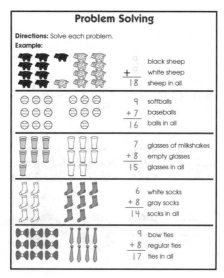

59

Hop Along Numbers

Directions: Use the number line to count back.

Example: 8, 7, 6

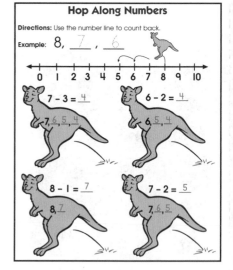

60

Your Total Solution for Math: Grade 2

Answer Key

Bubbly Baths

Directions: Solve the subtraction sentences below. Write each answer on a rubber duck.

61

Leaves Leaving the Limb

Directions: Subtract to find the difference. Use the code to color the leaves. Code: 0 = green 1 = red 2 = yellow 3 = brown

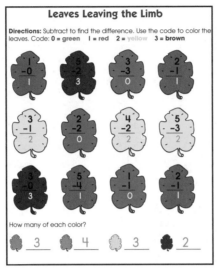

How many of each color?

3   4   3   2

62

Differences in Boxes

Directions: Color the two numbers in each box that show the given difference.

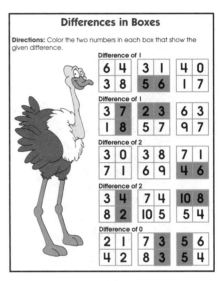

63

Subtraction Makes Al Tired

Directions: Write a different problem for each answer.

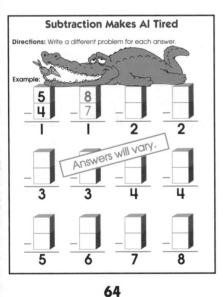

Answers will vary.

64

Looping Differences

Directions: Circle the two numbers next to each other that make the given difference. Find as many as you can in each row.

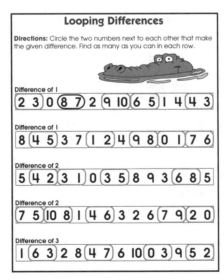

65

Hidden Differences of 2

Directions: Circle the pairs that have a difference of 2.

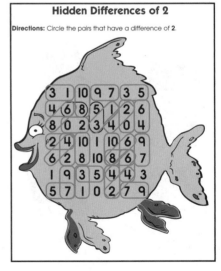

66

Answer Key

Hidden Differences of 3
Directions: Circle the pairs that have a difference of **3**.

67

Gone Fishing
Directions: Complete the subtraction sentences to make each problem correct.

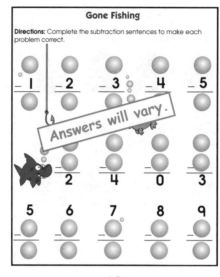

Answers will vary.

68

A Nose for Subtraction
Directions: Cut out the elephant heads at the bottom of the page. Glue each head on the body with the correct answer.

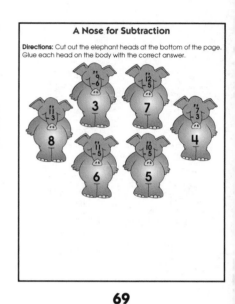

69

Crayon Count
Directions: Count the crayons. Write the number on the blank. Circle the problems that equal the answer.

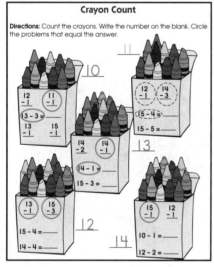

71

Subtraction Facts Through 12
Directions: Subtract.

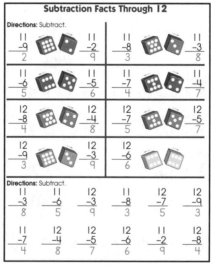

72

Subtraction Facts Through 18
Directions: Subtract.

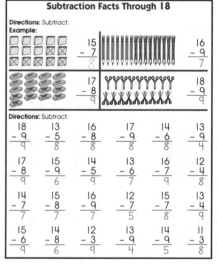

73

Your Total Solution for Math: Grade 2

Answer Key

"Grrreat" Picture

Directions: Subtract. Write the answer in the space. Then, color the spaces according to the answers.

1 = white   2 = purple   3 = black   4 = green   5 = yellow
6 = blue   7 = pink   8 = gray   9 = orange   10 = red

74

Connect the Facts

Directions: Solve the subtraction problems below.

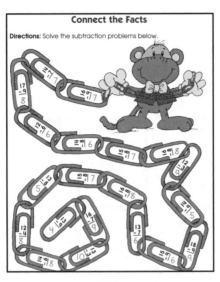

75

Swamp Stories

Directions: Read the story. Subtract to find the difference. Write the number in the box.

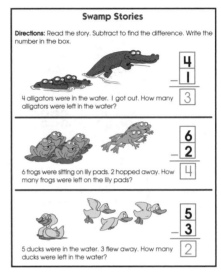

$$\begin{array}{r} 4 \\ -\ 1 \\ \hline 3 \end{array}$$

4 alligators were in the water. I got out. How many alligators were left in the water?

$$\begin{array}{r} 6 \\ -\ 2 \\ \hline 4 \end{array}$$

6 frogs were sitting on lily pads. 2 hopped away. How many frogs were left on the lily pads?

$$\begin{array}{r} 5 \\ -\ 3 \\ \hline 2 \end{array}$$

5 ducks were in the water. 3 flew away. How many ducks were left in the water?

76

More Animal Stories

Directions: Subtract to find the difference. Cut out the subtraction sentences and glue them in the correct boxes. Write the difference in each small box.

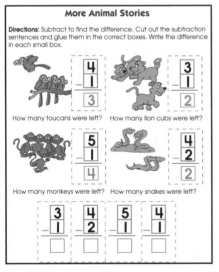

How many toucans were left?   How many lion cubs were left?

How many monkeys were left?   How many snakes were left?

77

Facts Through 5

Directions: Add or subtract.

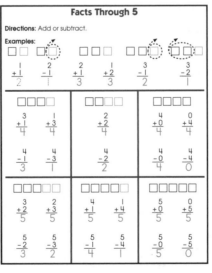

79

Facts for 6 and 7

Directions: Add or subtract.

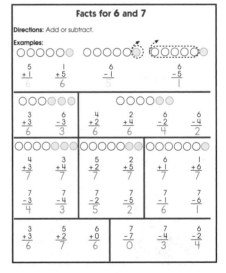

80

Answer Key

Facts for 8 — page 81

Directions: Add or subtract.

Examples:

$\begin{array}{r}5\\+3\\\hline 8\end{array}$ $\quad$ $\begin{array}{r}3\\+5\\\hline 8\end{array}$ $\quad$ $\begin{array}{r}8\\-3\\\hline 5\end{array}$ $\quad$ $\begin{array}{r}8\\-5\\\hline 3\end{array}$

$\begin{array}{r}4\\+4\\\hline 8\end{array}$ $\quad$ $\begin{array}{r}6\\+2\\\hline 8\end{array}$ $\quad$ $\begin{array}{r}2\\+6\\\hline 8\end{array}$ $\quad$ $\begin{array}{r}7\\+1\\\hline 8\end{array}$ $\quad$ $\begin{array}{r}1\\+7\\\hline 8\end{array}$

$\begin{array}{r}8\\-4\\\hline 4\end{array}$ $\quad$ $\begin{array}{r}8\\-2\\\hline 6\end{array}$ $\quad$ $\begin{array}{r}8\\-6\\\hline 2\end{array}$ $\quad$ $\begin{array}{r}8\\-1\\\hline 7\end{array}$ $\quad$ $\begin{array}{r}8\\-7\\\hline 1\end{array}$

$\begin{array}{r}2\\+6\\\hline 8\end{array}$ $\quad$ $\begin{array}{r}4\\+3\\\hline 7\end{array}$ $\quad$ $\begin{array}{r}5\\+1\\\hline 6\end{array}$ $\quad$ $\begin{array}{r}3\\+5\\\hline 8\end{array}$ $\quad$ $\begin{array}{r}7\\+1\\\hline 8\end{array}$ $\quad$ $\begin{array}{r}0\\+8\\\hline 8\end{array}$

$\begin{array}{r}8\\-1\\\hline 7\end{array}$ $\quad$ $\begin{array}{r}7\\-6\\\hline 1\end{array}$ $\quad$ $\begin{array}{r}8\\-5\\\hline 3\end{array}$ $\quad$ $\begin{array}{r}6\\-3\\\hline 3\end{array}$ $\quad$ $\begin{array}{r}8\\-0\\\hline 8\end{array}$ $\quad$ $\begin{array}{r}8\\-2\\\hline 6\end{array}$

81

Facts for 9 — page 82

Directions: Add or subtract.

Examples:

$\begin{array}{r}5\\+4\\\hline 9\end{array}$ $\quad$ $\begin{array}{r}4\\+5\\\hline 9\end{array}$ $\quad$ $\begin{array}{r}9\\-4\\\hline 5\end{array}$ $\quad$ $\begin{array}{r}9\\-5\\\hline 4\end{array}$

$\begin{array}{r}6\\+3\\\hline 9\end{array}$ $\quad$ $\begin{array}{r}3\\+6\\\hline 9\end{array}$ $\quad$ $\begin{array}{r}7\\+2\\\hline 9\end{array}$ $\quad$ $\begin{array}{r}2\\+7\\\hline 9\end{array}$ $\quad$ $\begin{array}{r}8\\+1\\\hline 9\end{array}$ $\quad$ $\begin{array}{r}1\\+8\\\hline 9\end{array}$

$\begin{array}{r}9\\-3\\\hline 6\end{array}$ $\quad$ $\begin{array}{r}9\\-6\\\hline 3\end{array}$ $\quad$ $\begin{array}{r}9\\-2\\\hline 7\end{array}$ $\quad$ $\begin{array}{r}9\\-7\\\hline 2\end{array}$ $\quad$ $\begin{array}{r}9\\-1\\\hline 8\end{array}$ $\quad$ $\begin{array}{r}9\\-8\\\hline 1\end{array}$

$\begin{array}{r}5\\+4\\\hline 9\end{array}$ $\quad$ $\begin{array}{r}2\\+7\\\hline 9\end{array}$ $\quad$ $\begin{array}{r}6\\+1\\\hline 7\end{array}$ $\quad$ $\begin{array}{r}9\\+0\\\hline 9\end{array}$ $\quad$ $\begin{array}{r}1\\+8\\\hline 9\end{array}$ $\quad$ $\begin{array}{r}4\\+4\\\hline 8\end{array}$

$\begin{array}{r}9\\-5\\\hline 4\end{array}$ $\quad$ $\begin{array}{r}7\\-3\\\hline 4\end{array}$ $\quad$ $\begin{array}{r}9\\-8\\\hline 1\end{array}$ $\quad$ $\begin{array}{r}9\\-3\\\hline 6\end{array}$ $\quad$ $\begin{array}{r}9\\-9\\\hline 0\end{array}$ $\quad$ $\begin{array}{r}9\\-0\\\hline 9\end{array}$

82

Facts for 10 — page 83

Directions: Add or subtract.

Examples:

$\begin{array}{r}5\\+5\\\hline 10\end{array}$ $\quad$ $\begin{array}{r}6\\+4\\\hline 10\end{array}$ $\quad$ $\begin{array}{r}4\\+6\\\hline 10\end{array}$ $\quad$ $\begin{array}{r}7\\+3\\\hline 10\end{array}$ $\quad$ $\begin{array}{r}3\\+7\\\hline 10\end{array}$

$\begin{array}{r}10\\-5\\\hline 5\end{array}$ $\quad$ $\begin{array}{r}10\\-4\\\hline 6\end{array}$ $\quad$ $\begin{array}{r}10\\-6\\\hline 4\end{array}$ $\quad$ $\begin{array}{r}10\\-3\\\hline 7\end{array}$

$\begin{array}{r}8\\+2\\\hline 10\end{array}$ $\quad$ $\begin{array}{r}2\\+8\\\hline 10\end{array}$ $\quad$ $\begin{array}{r}9\\+1\\\hline 10\end{array}$ $\quad$ $\begin{array}{r}1\\+9\\\hline 10\end{array}$

$\begin{array}{r}10\\-2\\\hline 8\end{array}$ $\quad$ $\begin{array}{r}10\\-8\\\hline 2\end{array}$ $\quad$ $\begin{array}{r}10\\-1\\\hline 9\end{array}$ $\quad$ $\begin{array}{r}10\\-9\\\hline 1\end{array}$

$\begin{array}{r}4\\+6\\\hline 10\end{array}$ $\quad$ $\begin{array}{r}5\\+5\\\hline 10\end{array}$ $\quad$ $\begin{array}{r}9\\+1\\\hline 10\end{array}$ $\quad$ $\begin{array}{r}10\\-8\\\hline 2\end{array}$ $\quad$ $\begin{array}{r}10\\-3\\\hline 7\end{array}$ $\quad$ $\begin{array}{r}10\\-0\\\hline 10\end{array}$

83

Problem Solving — page 84

Directions: Solve each problem.

Example:

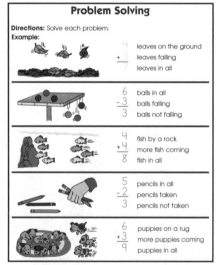

$\begin{array}{r}4\\+3\\\hline 7\end{array}$ leaves on the ground / leaves falling / leaves in all

$\begin{array}{r}6\\-3\\\hline 3\end{array}$ balls in all / balls falling / balls not falling

$\begin{array}{r}4\\+4\\\hline 8\end{array}$ fish by a rock / more fish coming / fish in all

$\begin{array}{r}5\\-2\\\hline 3\end{array}$ pencils in all / pencils taken / pencils not taken

$\begin{array}{r}6\\+3\\\hline 9\end{array}$ puppies on a rug / more puppies coming / puppies in all

84

Checkup — page 85

Directions: Add.

$\begin{array}{r}2\\+4\\\hline 6\end{array}$ $\quad$ $\begin{array}{r}7\\+3\\\hline 10\end{array}$ $\quad$ $\begin{array}{r}4\\+5\\\hline 9\end{array}$ $\quad$ $\begin{array}{r}6\\+2\\\hline 8\end{array}$ $\quad$ $\begin{array}{r}2\\+3\\\hline 5\end{array}$ $\quad$ $\begin{array}{r}4\\+0\\\hline 4\end{array}$

$\begin{array}{r}4\\+3\\\hline 7\end{array}$ $\quad$ $\begin{array}{r}1\\+5\\\hline 6\end{array}$ $\quad$ $\begin{array}{r}2\\+8\\\hline 10\end{array}$ $\quad$ $\begin{array}{r}3\\+3\\\hline 6\end{array}$ $\quad$ $\begin{array}{r}6\\+4\\\hline 10\end{array}$ $\quad$ $\begin{array}{r}2\\+1\\\hline 3\end{array}$

$\begin{array}{r}3\\+1\\\hline 4\end{array}$ $\quad$ $\begin{array}{r}7\\+0\\\hline 7\end{array}$ $\quad$ $\begin{array}{r}8\\+1\\\hline 9\end{array}$ $\quad$ $\begin{array}{r}5\\+2\\\hline 7\end{array}$ $\quad$ $\begin{array}{r}3\\+6\\\hline 9\end{array}$ $\quad$ $\begin{array}{r}5\\+5\\\hline 10\end{array}$

Directions: Subtract.

$\begin{array}{r}3\\-3\\\hline 0\end{array}$ $\quad$ $\begin{array}{r}5\\-2\\\hline 3\end{array}$ $\quad$ $\begin{array}{r}10\\-6\\\hline 4\end{array}$ $\quad$ $\begin{array}{r}9\\-2\\\hline 7\end{array}$ $\quad$ $\begin{array}{r}7\\-3\\\hline 4\end{array}$ $\quad$ $\begin{array}{r}10\\-5\\\hline 5\end{array}$

$\begin{array}{r}9\\-1\\\hline 8\end{array}$ $\quad$ $\begin{array}{r}8\\-7\\\hline 1\end{array}$ $\quad$ $\begin{array}{r}1\\-0\\\hline 1\end{array}$ $\quad$ $\begin{array}{r}6\\-4\\\hline 2\end{array}$ $\quad$ $\begin{array}{r}8\\-5\\\hline 3\end{array}$ $\quad$ $\begin{array}{r}10\\-8\\\hline 2\end{array}$

$\begin{array}{r}9\\-6\\\hline 3\end{array}$ $\quad$ $\begin{array}{r}4\\-3\\\hline 1\end{array}$ $\quad$ $\begin{array}{r}6\\-3\\\hline 3\end{array}$ $\quad$ $\begin{array}{r}7\\-5\\\hline 2\end{array}$ $\quad$ $\begin{array}{r}10\\-9\\\hline 1\end{array}$ $\quad$ $\begin{array}{r}8\\-4\\\hline 4\end{array}$

85

Addition and Subtraction — page 86

Directions: Solve the number problem under each picture. Write + or − to show if you should add or subtract.

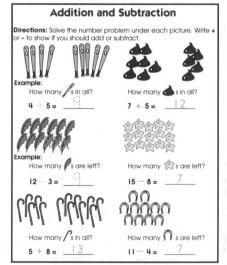

Example:

How many /s in all?

$4 + 5 = 9$

How many ◗s in all?

$7 + 5 = 12$

Example:

How many 🪶s are left?

$12 - 3 = 9$

How many ☆s are left?

$15 - 8 = 7$

How many /s in all?

$5 + 8 = 13$

How many ∩s are left?

$11 - 4 = 7$

86

Your Total Solution for Math: Grade 2

Answer Key

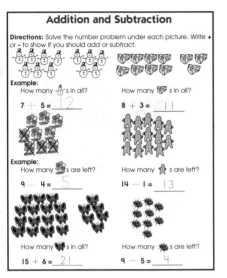

87

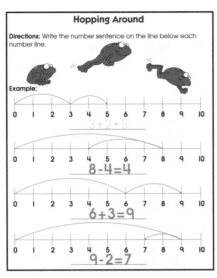

88

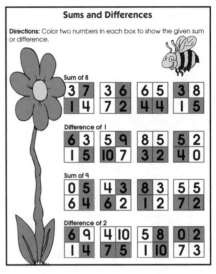

89

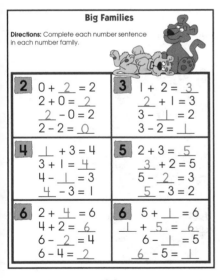

90

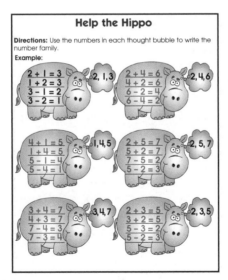

91

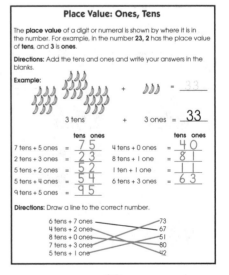

92

Answer Key

Finding Place Value: Ones and Tens

Directions: Write the numbers for the tens and ones. Then add.

Example:

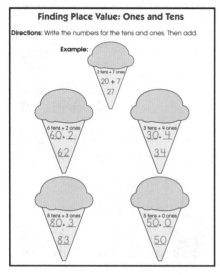

2 tens + 7 ones
20 + 7
27

6 tens + 2 ones
60 + 2
62

3 tens + 4 ones
30 + 4
34

8 tens + 3 ones
80 + 3
83

5 tens + 0 ones
50 + 0
50

93

Numbers 11 Through 18

1¢   10¢   10¢

Directions: Complete the problems.

Example:

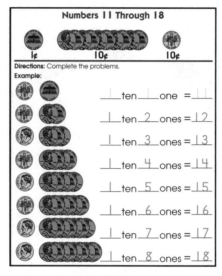

1 ten 1 one = 11
1 ten 2 ones = 12
1 ten 3 ones = 13
1 ten 4 ones = 14
1 ten 5 ones = 15
1 ten 6 ones = 16
1 ten 7 ones = 17
1 ten 8 ones = 18

94

Numbers 19 Through 39

Directions: Complete the problems.

Example:

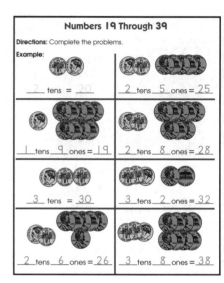

2 tens = 20   2 tens 5 ones = 25

1 tens 9 ones = 19   2 tens 8 ones = 28

3 tens = 30   3 tens 2 ones = 32

2 tens 6 ones = 26   3 tens 8 ones = 38

95

Numbers 40 Through 99

Directions: Complete the problems.

Example:

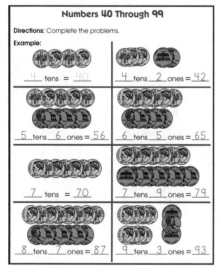

4 tens = 40   4 tens 2 ones = 42

5 tens 6 ones = 56   6 tens 5 ones = 65

7 tens = 70   7 tens 9 ones = 79

8 tens 7 ones = 87   9 tens 3 ones = 93

96

Numbers Through 99

Directions: Complete the problems.

Example:

4 tens 6 ones = 46	2 tens 1 one = 21
1 ten 2 ones = 12	5 tens 7 ones = 57
3 tens 7 ones = 37	1 ten 9 ones = 19
2 tens 4 ones = 24	8 tens 8 ones = 88
9 tens = 90	6 tens 7 ones = 67
6 tens = 60	7 tens 2 ones = 72
5 tens 3 ones = 53	9 tens 5 ones = 95
7 tens 8 ones = 78	4 tens 1 one = 41
1 ten 1 one = 11	3 tens 4 ones = 34
8 tens 4 ones = 84	6 tens 6 ones = 66
3 tens 5 ones = 35	8 tens 9 ones = 89
4 tens 9 ones = 49	2 tens = 20
9 tens 6 ones = 96	5 tens = 50

97

Hundreds, Tens, and Ones

Directions: Count the groups of crayons. Write the number of hundreds, tens, and ones.

Example:

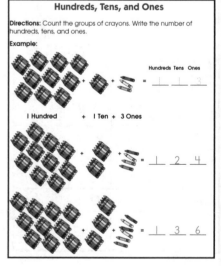

Hundreds Tens Ones

= 1   1   3

1 Hundred + 1 Ten + 3 Ones

= 1   2   4

= 1   3   6

98

Your Total Solution for Math: Grade 2

Answer Key

What Big Numbers!

Directions: Write each number.

Example:

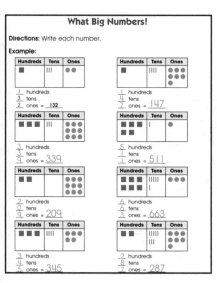

Hundreds	Tens	Ones
■	|||	●●

_1_ hundreds
_3_ tens
_2_ ones = _132_

Hundreds	Tens	Ones
■	||||	●●●●●

_1_ hundreds
_4_ tens
_7_ ones = _147_

Hundreds	Tens	Ones
■■■	|||	●●●●

_3_ hundreds
_3_ tens
_9_ ones = _339_

Hundreds	Tens	Ones
■	|||||	

_5_ hundreds
_1_ tens
_1_ ones = _511_

Hundreds	Tens	Ones
■■		●●●

_2_ hundreds
_0_ tens
_9_ ones = _209_

Hundreds	Tens	Ones
■■	|||||	●●●

_6_ hundreds
_6_ tens
_3_ ones = _663_

Hundreds	Tens	Ones
■■■	||||	●●●●

_3_ hundreds
_4_ tens
_5_ ones = _345_

Hundreds	Tens	Ones
■■	|||||	●●●

_2_ hundreds
_8_ tens
_7_ ones = _287_

99

Count 'Em Up!

Directions: Look at the example. Then, write the missing numbers in the blanks.

Example:

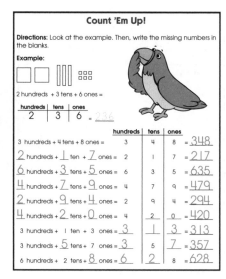

2 hundreds + 3 tens + 6 ones =

hundreds	tens	ones
2	3	6	= _236_

	hundreds	tens	ones	
3 hundreds + 4 tens + 8 ones =	3	4	8	= _348_
_2_ hundreds + _1_ ten + _7_ ones =	2	1	7	= _217_
_6_ hundreds + _3_ tens + _5_ ones =	6	3	5	= _635_
_4_ hundreds + _7_ tens + _9_ ones =	4	7	9	= _479_
_2_ hundreds + _9_ tens + _4_ ones =	2	9	4	= _294_
_4_ hundreds + _2_ tens + _0_ ones =	4	2	0	= _420_
3 hundreds + 1 ten + 3 ones =	_3_	_1_	_3_	= _313_
3 hundreds + _5_ tens + 7 ones =	_3_	5	_7_	= _357_
6 hundreds + 2 tens + _8_ ones =	_6_	_2_	8	= _628_

100

Up, Up, and Away

Directions: Use the code to color the balloons. If the answer has:

7 hundreds, color it red.
6 hundreds, color it green.
5 hundreds, color it orange.
8 tens, color it yellow.
3 ones, color it brown.

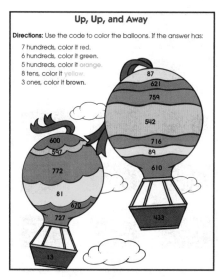

101

Place Value: Thousands

Directions: Study the example. Write the missing numbers.

Example:

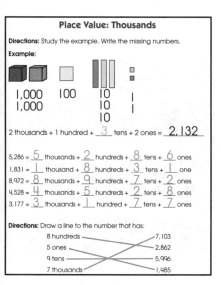

1,000   100   10   1
1,000   10   1
                 10

2 thousands + 1 hundred + _3_ tens + 2 ones = _2,132_

5,286 = _5_ thousands + _2_ hundreds + _8_ tens + _6_ ones
1,831 = _1_ thousand + _8_ hundreds + _3_ tens + _1_ one
8,972 = _8_ thousands + _9_ hundreds + _7_ tens + _2_ ones
4,528 = _4_ thousands + _5_ hundreds + _2_ tens + _8_ ones
3,177 = _3_ thousands + _1_ hundred + _7_ tens + _7_ ones

Directions: Draw a line to the number that has:

8 hundreds —— 7,103
5 ones —— 2,862
9 tens —— 5,996
7 thousands —— 1,485

102

Place Value: Thousands

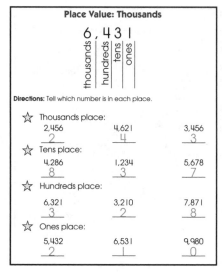

6 , 4 3 1
thousands | hundreds | tens | ones

Directions: Tell which number is in each place.

☆ Thousands place:

2,456   4,621   3,456
_2_   _4_   _3_

☆ Tens place:

4,286   1,234   5,678
_8_   _3_   _7_

☆ Hundreds place:

6,321   3,210   7,871
_3_   _2_   _8_

☆ Ones place:

5,432   6,531   9,980
_2_   _1_   _0_

103

Two-Digit Addition

Directions: Study the example. Follow the steps to add.

Example:
33
+41

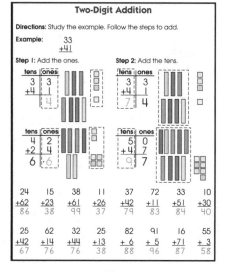

Step 1: Add the ones.

tens	ones
3	3
+4	1
	4

Step 2: Add the tens.

tens	ones
3	3
+4	1
7	4

tens	ones
4	2
+2	4
6	6

tens	ones
5	0
+4	7
9	7

24	15	38	11	37	72	33	10
+62	+23	+61	+26	+42	+11	+51	+30
86	38	99	37	79	83	84	40

25	62	32	25	82	91	16	55
+42	+14	+44	+13	+ 6	+ 5	+71	+ 3
67	76	76	38	88	96	87	58

104

Answer Key

Two-Digit Addition

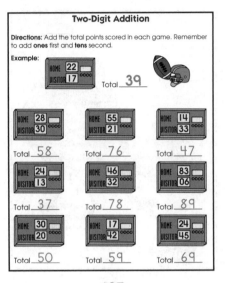

Directions: Add the total points scored in each game. Remember to add **ones** first and **tens** second.

Example:

HOME 22 / VISITOR 17   Total **39**

HOME 28 / VISITOR 30   Total **58**
HOME 55 / VISITOR 21   Total **76**
HOME 14 / VISITOR 33   Total **47**

HOME 24 / VISITOR 13   Total **37**
HOME 46 / VISITOR 32   Total **78**
HOME 83 / VISITOR 06   Total **89**

HOME 30 / VISITOR 20   Total **50**
HOME 17 / VISITOR 42   Total **59**
HOME 24 / VISITOR 45   Total **69**

105

Adding Tens

3 tens	30	6 tens	60
+ 4 tens	+40	+ 2 tens	+20
7 tens	70	8 tens	80

Directions: Add.

2 tens	20	6 tens	60
+ 4 tens	+40	+ 2 tens	+20
6 tens	60	8 tens	80

20	10	40	30	50
+20	+50	+20	+40	+30
40	60	60	70	80

30	60	20	70	10
+20	+10	+50	+10	+10
50	70	70	80	20

10	40	80	60	20
+20	+40	+10	+30	+60
30	80	90	90	80

70	40	30	50	30
+20	+10	+10	+40	+30
90	50	40	90	60

106

Problem Solving

Directions: Solve each problem.

Example:

There are 20 men in the plane.
30 women get in the plane.
How many men and women are in the plane?
20 + 30 = **50**

Jill buys 10 apples.
Carol buys 20 apples.
How many apples in all?
10 + 20 = **30**

There are 30 ears of corn in one pile.
There are 50 ears of corn in another pile.
How many ears of corn in all?
30 + 50 = **80**

Henry cut 40 pieces of wood.
Art cut 20 pieces of wood.
How many pieces of wood were cut?
40 + 20 = **60**

Adolpho had 60 baseball cards.
Maria had 30 baseball cards.
How many baseball cards in all?
60 + 30 = **90**

107

Digital Addition

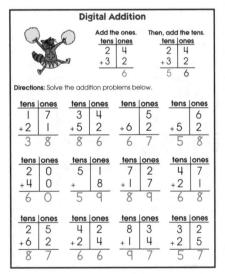

Add the ones.
tens	ones
2	4
+3	2
	6

Then, add the tens.
tens	ones
2	4
+3	2
5	6

Directions: Solve the addition problems below.

tens	ones
1	7
+2	1
3	8

tens	ones
3	4
+5	2
8	6

tens	ones
	5
+6	2
6	7

tens	ones
	6
+5	2
5	8

tens	ones
2	0
+4	0
6	0

tens	ones
5	1
+	8
5	9

tens	ones
7	2
+1	7
8	9

tens	ones
4	7
+2	1
6	8

tens	ones
2	5
+6	2
8	7

tens	ones
4	2
+2	4
6	6

tens	ones
8	3
+1	4
9	7

tens	ones
3	2
+2	5
5	7

108

Circus Fun

Directions: Add to solve the problems. Add the ones first. Then, add the tens.

tens	ones
2	5
+1	4
3	9

tens	ones
5	3
+3	2
8	5

tens	ones
7	1
+2	8
9	9

tens	ones
4	4
+3	2
7	6

tens	ones
5	1
+3	7
8	8

tens	ones
2	6
+5	2
7	8

tens	ones
2	6
+4	2
6	8

tens	ones
3	7
+5	1
8	8

tens	ones
1	9
+3	0
4	9

109

Scoreboard Sums

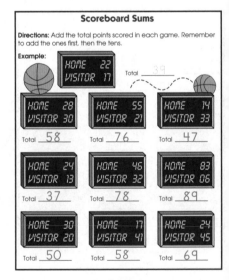

Directions: Add the total points scored in each game. Remember to add the ones first, then the tens.

Example:

HOME 22 / VISITOR 17   Total **39**

HOME 28 / VISITOR 30   Total **58**
HOME 55 / VISITOR 21   Total **76**
HOME 14 / VISITOR 33   Total **47**

HOME 24 / VISITOR 13   Total **37**
HOME 46 / VISITOR 32   Total **78**
HOME 83 / VISITOR 06   Total **89**

HOME 30 / VISITOR 20   Total **50**
HOME 17 / VISITOR 41   Total **58**
HOME 24 / VISITOR 45   Total **69**

110

Your Total Solution for Math: Grade 2

Answer Key

111

Two-Digit Subtraction

Directions: Look at the example. Follow the steps to subtract.

Examples: 28   24
−14 −12

Step 1: Subtract the ones.

tens	ones
2	8
−1	4
	4

Step 2: Subtract the tens.

tens	ones
2	8
−1	4
1	4

Step 1: Subtract the ones.

tens	ones
2	4
−1	2
	2

Step 2: Subtract the tens.

tens	ones
2	4
−1	2
1	2

24	61	77	85	57	87
−12	−30	−44	−24	−23	−33
12	31	33	61	34	54

112

Subtracting Tens

Examples:

6 tens	60		8 tens	80
−3 tens	−30		−2 tens	−20
3 tens	30		6 tens	60

Directions: Subtract.

7 tens	70		4 tens	40
−5 tens	−50		−2 tens	−20
2 tens	20		2 tens	20

50	60	20	80	40
−30	−20	−10	−40	−40
20	40	10	40	0

90	80	70	30	50
−50	−20	−30	−20	−40
40	60	40	10	10

60	40	80	90	70
−30	−10	−30	−20	−50
30	30	50	70	20

80	90	70	60	50
−70	−80	−40	−40	−20
10	10	30	20	30

113

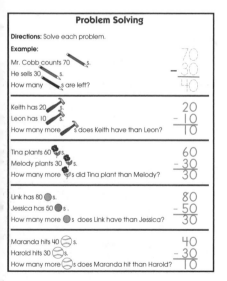

114

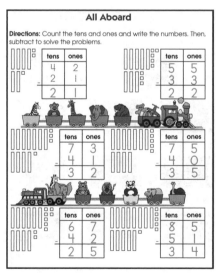

115

Cookie Mania

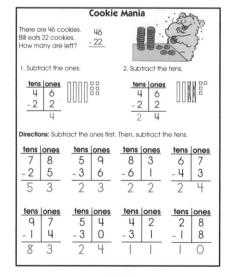

There are 46 cookies. Bill eats 22 cookies. How many are left?

46
−22

1. Subtract the ones.

tens	ones
4	6
−2	2
	4

2. Subtract the tens.

tens	ones
4	6
−2	2
2	4

Directions: Subtract the ones first. Then, subtract the tens.

tens	ones		tens	ones		tens	ones		tens	ones
7	8		5	9		8	3		6	7
−2	5		−3	6		−6	1		−4	3
5	3		2	3		2	2		2	4

tens	ones		tens	ones		tens	ones		tens	ones
9	7		5	4		4	2		2	8
−1	4		−3	0		−3	1		−1	8
8	3		2	4		1	1		1	0

116

Answer Key

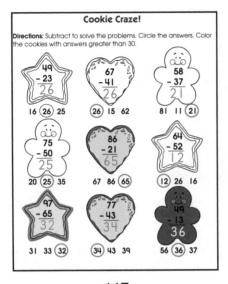

Cookie Craze!

Directions: Subtract to solve the problems. Circle the answers. Color the cookies with answers greater than 30.

49 − 23 = 26 → 16 (26) 25
67 − 41 = 26 → (26) 15 62
58 − 37 = 21 → 81 11 (21)
75 − 50 = 25 → 20 (25) 35
86 − 21 = 65 → 67 86 (65)
64 − 52 = 12 → (12) 26 16
97 − 65 = 32 → 31 33 (32)
77 − 43 = 34 → (34) 43 39
49 − 13 = 36 → 56 (36) 37

117

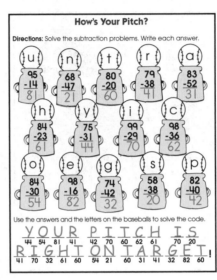

How's Your Pitch?

Directions: Solve the subtraction problems. Write each answer.

u) 95 − 14 = 81
n) 68 − 47 = 21
t) 80 − 20 = 60
r) 79 − 38 = 41
a) 83 − 52 = 31
h) 84 − 23 = 61
y) 75 − 31 = 44
i) 99 − 29 = 70
c) 98 − 36 = 62
o) 84 − 30 = 54
e) 98 − 16 = 82
g) 74 − 42 = 32
s) 58 − 38 = 20
p) 82 − 40 = 42

Use the answers and the letters on the baseballs to solve the code.

YOUR PITCH IS
44 70 32 61 60   54 21   60 31 41

RIGHT ON TARGET!
41 70 32 61 60   54 21   60 31 41 32 82 60

118

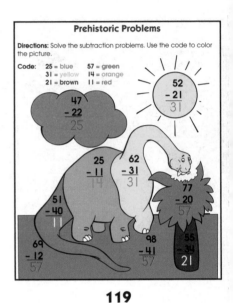

Prehistoric Problems

Directions: Solve the subtraction problems. Use the code to color the picture.

Code: 25 = blue   57 = green
31 = yellow   14 = orange
21 = brown   11 = red

52 − 21 = 31
47 − 22 = 25
25 − 11 = 14
62 − 31 = 31
77 − 20 = 57
51 − 40 = 11
69 − 12 = 57
98 − 41 = 57
55 − 34 = 21

119

Two-Digit Addition: Regrouping

Addition is "putting together" or adding two or more numbers to find the sum. Regrouping is using **ten ones** to form **one ten, ten tens** to form **one 100, fifteen ones** to form **one ten** and **five ones,** and so on.

Directions: Study the examples. Follow the steps to add.

Example: 14 + 8

Step 1: Add the ones.
tens | ones
1 | 4
+ | 8
  | 12

Step 2: Regroup the tens.
tens | ones
1 | 4
+ | 8
  | 2

Step 3: Add the tens.
tens | ones
1 | 4
+ | 8
2 | 2

tens | ones
1 | 6
+3 | 7
5 | 3

tens | ones
3 | 8
+5 | 1
9 | 1

tens | ones
2 | 4
+4 | 7
7 | 1

28 +17 = 45
32 +38 = 70
54 +25 = 79
19 +55 = 74
44 +48 = 92
25 +64 = 89
29 +33 = 62
79 +15 = 94

120

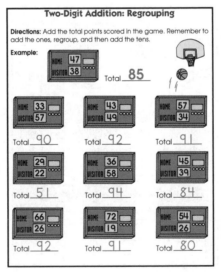

Two-Digit Addition: Regrouping

Directions: Add the total points scored in the game. Remember to add the ones, regroup, and then add the tens.

Example:
HOME 47
VISITOR 38
Total 85

HOME 33 / VISITOR 57 — Total 90
HOME 43 / VISITOR 49 — Total 92
HOME 57 / VISITOR 34 — Total 91
HOME 29 / VISITOR 22 — Total 51
HOME 36 / VISITOR 58 — Total 94
HOME 45 / VISITOR 39 — Total 84
HOME 66 / VISITOR 26 — Total 92
HOME 72 / VISITOR 19 — Total 91
HOME 54 / VISITOR 26 — Total 80

121

Two-Digit Addition

Directions: Add the ones.   Rename 15 as 10 + 5.   Add the tens.

56 + 29   6 + 9 = 15 or 10 + 5   56 + 29 → 5   56 + 29 = 85

Directions: Add the ones.   Rename 12 as 10 + 2.   Add the tens.

47 + 35   7 + 5 = 12 or 10 + 2   47 + 35 → 2   47 + 35 = 82

Directions: Add.

Examples:

45 +28 = 73
13 +19 = 32
48 +35 = 83
69 +18 = 87
54 +39 = 93

44 +17 = 61
37 +18 = 55
28 +36 = 64
73 +18 = 91
66 +29 = 95

52 +39 = 91
38 +47 = 85
64 +18 = 82
29 +45 = 74
75 +17 = 92

122

Your Total Solution for Math: Grade 2

Answer Key

Two-Digit Addition

Directions: Add the ones.　Rename 11 as 10 + 1.　Add the tens.

```
  3 8          8            3 8           3 8
+ 4 3        + 3          + 4 3         + 4 3
             11 or 10 + 1                 8 1
```

Directions: Add.

Example:

17 + 34 51	26 + 47 73	47 + 35 82	68 + 24 92	37 + 28 65
29 + 48 77	58 + 27 85	69 + 17 86	78 + 13 91	19 + 44 63
55 + 28 83	27 + 35 62	39 + 52 91	57 + 27 84	38 + 36 74
49 + 43 92	65 + 18 83	23 + 18 41	64 + 18 82	46 + 39 85
54 + 27 81	38 + 44 82	66 + 26 92	28 + 34 62	19 + 56 75

123

Two-Digit Subtraction: Regrouping

Subtraction is "taking away" or subtracting one number from another to find the difference. Regrouping is using **one ten** to form **ten ones**, **one 100** to form **ten tens**, and so on.

Directions: Study the examples. Follow the steps to subtract.

Example: 37 − 19

Step 1: Regroup.　**Step 2:** Subtract the ones.　**Step 3:** Subtract the tens.

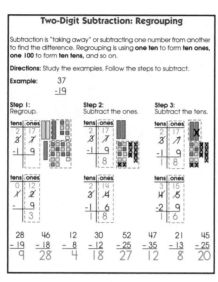

28 − 19 9	46 − 18 28	12 − 8 4	30 − 12 18	52 − 25 27	47 − 35 12	21 − 13 8

45 − 25 = 20

124

Two-Digit Subtraction: Regrouping

Directions: Study the steps for subtracting. Solve the problems using the steps.

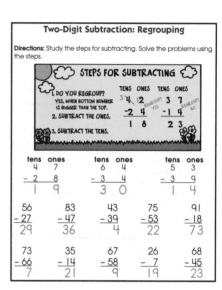

tens ones	tens ones	tens ones
4　7 − 2　8 1　9	6　4 − 3　4 3　0	5　3 − 3　9 1　4

56 − 27 29	83 − 47 36	43 − 39 4	75 − 53 22	91 − 18 73
73 − 66 7	35 − 14 21	67 − 58 9	26 − 7 19	68 − 45 23

125

Subtraction With Regrouping

Directions: Use manipulatives to find the difference.

Example:

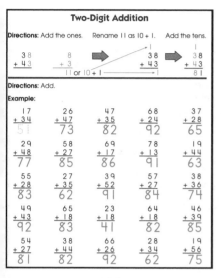

127

Two-Digit Subtraction

Directions: Rename 53 as 4 tens and 13 ones.　Subtract the ones.　Subtract the tens.

```
  4 13        4 13        4 13
  5 3    →    5 3    →    5 3
− 2 6       − 2 6       − 2 6
              7          2 7
```

Rename 45 as 3 tens and 15 ones.

```
  3 15       3 15       3 15
  4 5    →   4 5    →   4 5
− 1 8      − 1 8      − 1 8
             7         2 7
```

Directions: Subtract.

Examples:

5 13 6 3 − 2 8 35	6 14 7 4 − 3 9 35	47 − 28 19	52 − 26 26	64 − 36 28
84 − 47 37	93 − 56 37	71 − 23 48	26 − 18 8	67 − 48 19
44 − 28 16	53 − 37 16	82 − 46 36	94 − 66 28	55 − 39 16
86 − 58 28	34 − 18 16	54 − 29 25	73 − 59 14	86 − 69 17

128

Two-Digit Subtraction

Directions: Rename 73 as 6 tens and 13 ones.　Subtract the ones.　Subtract the tens.

```
  6 13       6 13       6 13
  7 3    →   7 3    →   7 3
− 4 8      − 4 8      − 4 8
             5         2 5
```

Directions: Subtract.

Example:

5 13 6 3 − 4 8 15	83 − 45 38	74 − 29 45	94 − 48 46	62 − 25 37
45 − 27 18	33 − 24 9	24 − 8 6	86 − 37 49	72 − 48 24
36 − 17 19	26 − 18 8	43 − 19 24	63 − 48 15	93 − 18 75
82 − 26 56	73 − 28 45	95 − 69 26	57 − 38 19	41 − 25 16
54 − 18 36	61 − 34 27	91 − 37 54	81 − 44 37	32 − 15 17

129

Answer Key

Problem Solving

Directions: Solve each problem.

Example:
Dad cooks 23 potatoes.
He uses 19 potatoes in the potato salad.
How many potatoes are left?
$23 - 19 = 4$

Susan draws 32 butterflies.
She colored 15 of them brown.
How many butterflies does she have left to color?
$32 - 15 = 17$

A book has 66 pages.
Pedro reads 39 pages.
How many pages are left to read?
$66 - 39 = 27$

Jerry picks up 34 seashells.
He puts 15 of them in a box.
How many does he have left?
$34 - 15 = 19$

Beth buys 72 sheets of paper.
She uses 44 sheets for her school work.
How many sheets of paper are left?
$72 - 44 = 28$

130

Addition and Subtraction Review

Directions: Add.

4 + 9 = 13	8 + 6 = 14	9 + 8 = 17	7 + 6 = 13	5 + 7 = 12	6 + 5 = 11
9 + 6 = 15	5 + 8 = 13	7 + 4 = 11	9 + 9 = 18	8 + 7 = 15	7 + 9 = 16
30 + 40 = 70	20 + 30 = 50	45 + 23 = 68	52 + 23 = 75	60 + 25 = 85	83 + 15 = 98

Directions: Subtract.

16 − 7 = 9	15 − 9 = 6	13 − 4 = 9	12 − 7 = 5	11 − 9 = 2	17 − 8 = 9
18 − 9 = 9	17 − 9 = 8	16 − 8 = 8	15 − 8 = 7	14 − 7 = 7	16 − 9 = 7
40 − 30 = 10	60 − 10 = 50	85 − 23 = 62	73 − 41 = 32	96 − 43 = 53	54 − 44 = 10

131

Review Two-Digit Addition

Directions: Add the ones. Rename 12 as 10 + 2. Add the tens.

64 + 28 → 4 + 8 = 12 or 10 + 2 → 64 + 28 = 92

Directions: Add.

Example:

28 + 19 = 47	34 + 49 = 83	25 + 16 = 41	46 + 29 = 75	54 + 39 = 93
16 + 39 = 55	64 + 28 = 92	58 + 24 = 82	39 + 17 = 56	34 + 19 = 53
57 + 39 = 96	14 + 48 = 62	37 + 39 = 76	61 + 19 = 80	29 + 44 = 73
17 + 35 = 52	39 + 14 = 53	44 + 37 = 81	25 + 49 = 74	18 + 18 = 36
26 + 48 = 74	39 + 27 = 66	14 + 27 = 41	65 + 25 = 90	59 + 18 = 77

132

Keep on Truckin'

Directions: Write each sum. Connect the sums of 83 to make a road for the truck.

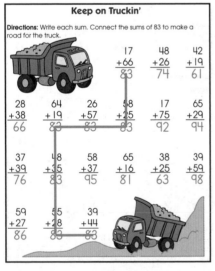

			17 + 66 = 83	48 + 26 = 74	42 + 19 = 61
28 + 38 = 66	64 + 19 = 83	26 + 57 = 83	58 + 25 = 83	17 + 75 = 92	65 + 29 = 94
37 + 39 = 76	48 + 35 = 83	58 + 37 = 95	65 + 16 = 81	38 + 25 = 63	39 + 59 = 98
59 + 27 = 86	55 + 28 = 83	39 + 44 = 83			

133

Review Two-Digit Subtraction

Directions: Rename 61 as 5 tens and 11 ones. Subtract the ones. Subtract the tens.

61 − 43 → 5 11 → 8 → 18

Directions: Subtract.

Example:
$47 - 28 = 19$

47 − 28 = 19	73 − 48 = 25	84 − 66 = 18	95 − 18 = 77	64 − 29 = 35
56 − 38 = 18	31 − 15 = 16	25 − 17 = 8	33 − 19 = 14	46 − 29 = 17
93 − 64 = 29	82 − 55 = 27	72 − 14 = 58	45 − 28 = 17	61 − 23 = 38
51 − 44 = 7	62 − 48 = 14	37 − 19 = 18	50 − 32 = 18	83 − 47 = 36
92 − 73 = 19	82 − 75 = 7	76 − 38 = 38	47 − 29 = 18	74 − 39 = 35

134

Review Two-Digit Subtraction

Directions: Subtract.

85 − 16 = 69	93 − 48 = 45	72 − 35 = 37	63 − 27 = 36	43 − 38 = 5
56 − 29 = 27	75 − 49 = 26	84 − 38 = 46	91 − 65 = 26	37 − 18 = 19
21 − 14 = 7	35 − 18 = 17	42 − 29 = 13	72 − 47 = 25	81 − 54 = 27
64 − 38 = 26	53 − 28 = 25	94 − 57 = 37	48 − 39 = 9	23 − 18 = 5
74 − 58 = 16	83 − 36 = 47	62 − 26 = 36	54 − 28 = 26	32 − 17 = 15

135

Your Total Solution for Math: Grade 2

Answer Key

Go "Fore" It!

Directions: Add or subtract using regrouping.

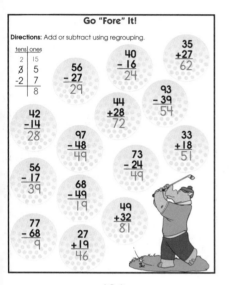

tens	ones
2	15
3̶	5̶
-2	7
	8

56 − 27 = 29

42 − 14 = 28

56 − 17 = 39

77 − 68 = 9

40 − 16 = 24

44 + 28 = 72

97 − 48 = 49

73 − 24 = 49

68 − 49 = 19

49 + 32 = 81

27 + 19 = 46

35 + 27 = 62

93 − 39 = 54

33 + 18 = 51

136

Monster Math

Directions: Add or subtract using regrouping.

84 − 56 = 28

41 − 17 = 24

52 − 28 = 24

72 − 19 = 53

84 − 27 = 57

57 − 39 = 18

33 − 15 = 18

64 + 17 = 81

36 − 19 = 17

65 − 28 = 37

48 − 30 = 18

33 + 18 = 51

25 + 35 = 60

137

Adding Hundreds

Examples:

5 hundreds	500	4 hundreds	400
+ 3 hundreds	+ 300	+ 5 hundreds	+ 500
8 hundreds	800	9 hundreds	900

Directions: Add.

3 hundreds	300	6 hundreds	600
+ 1 hundreds	+ 100	+ 2 hundreds	+ 200
4 hundreds	400	8 hundreds	800

200 + 200 = 400

100 + 700 = 800

600 + 300 = 900

400 + 500 = 900

300 + 400 = 700

800 + 100 = 900

400 + 400 = 800

700 + 200 = 900

500 + 100 = 600

100 + 600 = 700

500 + 200 = 700

300 + 200 = 500

300 + 300 = 600

400 + 200 = 600

300 + 500 = 800

200 + 100 = 300

138

Problem Solving

Directions: Solve each problem.

Example:

Ria packed 300 boxes.
Melvin packed 200 boxes.
How many boxes did Ria and Melvin pack?
300 + 200 = 500

Santo typed 500 letters.
Hale typed 400 letters.
How many letters did they type?
500 + 400 = 900

Paula used 100 paper clips.
Milton used 600 paper clips.
How many paper clips did they use?
100 + 600 = 700

The grocery store sold 400 red apples.
The grocery store also sold 100 yellow apples.
How many apples did the grocery store sell in all?
400 + 100 = 500

Miles worked 200 days.
Julia worked 500 days.
How many days did they work?
200 + 500 = 700

139

Three-Digit Addition

2 4 5		2 4 5		2 4 5
+ 2 5 3	→	+ 2 5 3	→	+ 2 5 3
8		9 8		4 9 8

Directions: Add.

Example:

7 4 5	6 2 3
+ 2 3	+ 1 5 6
7 6 8	7 7 9

Add the ones.
Add the tens.
Add the hundreds.

415 + 342 = 757

566 + 33 = 599

373 + 221 = 594

160 + 334 = 494

835 + 42 = 877

642 + 251 = 893

287 + 412 = 699

723 + 45 = 768

133 + 522 = 655

454 + 324 = 778

314 + 602 = 916

654 + 235 = 889

140

Problem Solving

Directions: Solve each problem.

Example:

Gene collected 342 rocks.
Lester collected 201 rocks.
How many rocks did they collect?
342 + 201 = 543

Tina jumped the rope 403 times.
Henry jumped the rope 426 times.
How many times did they jump?
403 + 426 = 829

There are 210 people wearing blue hats.
There are 432 people wearing red hats.
How many hats in all?
210 + 432 = 642

Asta used 135 paper plates.
Clyde used 143 paper plates.
How many paper plates did they use in all?
135 + 143 = 278

Aunt Mary had 536 dollars.
Uncle Lewis had 423 dollars.
How many dollars did they have in all?
536 + 423 = 959

141

Answer Key

Subtracting Hundreds

8 hundreds	800	6 hundreds	600
− 3 hundreds	− 300	− 2 hundreds	− 200
5 hundreds	500	4 hundreds	400

Directions: Subtract.

Example:

9 hundreds	900	3 hundreds	300
− 7 hundreds	− 700	− 1 hundreds	− 100
2 hundreds	200	2 hundreds	200

700	500	900	800
− 300	− 400	− 400	− 500
400	100	500	300

600	300	500	400
− 500	− 200	− 100	− 200
100	100	400	200

900	800	600	500
− 100	− 400	− 200	− 300
800	400	400	200

400	700	800	900
− 100	− 600	− 200	− 600
300	100	600	300

142

Problem Solving

Directions: Solve each problem.

Example:

There were 400 apples in a box.
Jesse took 100 apples from the box.
How many apples are still in the box?
400 − 100 = 300

Tommy bought 300 golf balls.
He gave Irene 200 golf balls.
How many golf balls does he have left?
300 − 200 = 100

The black horse ran 900 feet.
The brown horse ran 700 feet.
How many more feet did the black horse run?
900 − 700 = 200

The paint store has 800 gallons of paint.
It sells 300 gallons of paint.
How many gallons of paint are left?
800 − 300 = 500

There are 700 children.
There are 200 boys.
How many girls are there?
700 − 200 = 500

143

Three-Digit Subtraction

Directions: Subtract the ones. Subtract the tens. Subtract the hundreds.

746	746	746
− 424	− 424	− 424
2	22	322

Directions: Add.

Example:

879	586
− 46	− 142
833	444

Subtract the ones.
Subtract the tens.
Subtract the hundreds.

635	478	338	957
− 423	− 241	− 27	− 734
212	237	311	223

297	846	769	653
− 145	− 325	− 514	− 142
152	521	255	511

569	365	818	936
− 333	− 213	− 618	− 424
236	152	200	512

144

Problem Solving

Directions: Solve each problem.

Example:

There were 787 bales of hay.
Glenda fed the cows 535 bales.
How many bales of hay are left?
787 − 535 = 252

There are 673 bolts in a box.
Maria took 341 bolts out of the box.
How many bolts are left in the box?
673 − 341 = 332

The secretary types 459 letters.
138 of the letters were mailed.
How many letters are left?
459 − 138 = 321

Mr. Jones had 569 dollars.
He spent 203 dollars.
How many dollars does he have left?
569 − 203 = 366

There are 342 riding horses in the rodeo.
There are 132 bucking horses in the rodeo.
How many more riding horses are there?
342 − 132 = 210

145

Review: Three-Digit Addition

Directions: Add.

Examples:

340	754	826	632
+ 225	+ 32	+ 3	+ 322
565	786	829	954

198	456	541	273
+ 200	+ 31	+ 333	+ 415
398	487	874	688

900	847	721	402
+ 34	+ 131	+ 176	+ 383
934	978	897	785

156	644	215	372
+ 423	+ 251	+ 542	+ 417
579	895	757	789

518	783	684	710
+ 351	+ 5	+ 14	+ 260
869	788	698	970

146

Review: Three-Digit Subtraction

Directions: Subtract.

Example:

856	432	598	769
− 352	− 21	− 416	− 345
504	411	182	424

319	954	275	643
− 6	− 731	− 3	− 313
313	223	272	330

775	834	942	478
− 261	− 12	− 111	− 324
514	822	831	154

562	444	385	754
− 431	− 212	− 152	− 3
131	232	233	751

868	943	689	577
− 234	− 843	− 417	− 37
634	100	272	540

147

Your Total Solution for Math: Grade 2

Answer Key

Multiplication

Multiplication is a short way to find the sum of adding the same number a certain amount of times. For example, 7 x 4 = 28 instead of 7 + 7 + 7 + 7 = 28.

Directions: Study the example. Solve the problems.

Example:
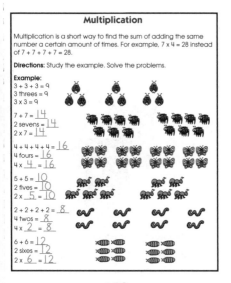
3 + 3 + 3 = 9
3 threes = 9
3 x 3 = 9

7 + 7 = 14
2 sevens = 14
2 x 7 = 14

4 + 4 + 4 + 4 = 16
4 fours = 16
4 x 4 = 16

5 + 5 = 10
2 fives = 10
2 x 5 = 10

2 + 2 + 2 + 2 = 8
4 twos = 8
4 x 2 = 8

6 + 6 = 12
2 sixes = 12
2 x 6 = 12

148

Multiplication

Multiplication is repeated addition.

Directions: Draw a picture for each problem. Then, write the missing numbers.

Example:
Draw 2 groups of three apples.

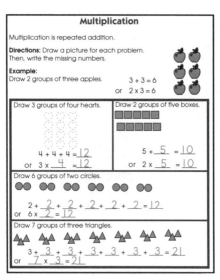

3 + 3 = 6
or 2 x 3 = 6

Draw 3 groups of four hearts.

4 + 4 + 4 = 12
or 3 x 4 = 12

Draw 2 groups of five boxes.

5 + 5 = 10
or 2 x 5 = 10

Draw 6 groups of two circles.

2 + 2 + 2 + 2 + 2 + 2 = 12
or 6 x 2 = 12

Draw 7 groups of three triangles.

3 + 3 + 3 + 3 + 3 + 3 + 3 = 21
or 7 x 3 = 21

149

Multiplication

Directions: Study the example. Draw the groups and write the total.

Example: 3 x 2
2 + 2 + 2 = 6

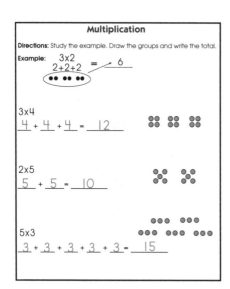

3 x 4
4 + 4 + 4 = 12

2 x 5
5 + 5 = 10

5 x 3
3 + 3 + 3 + 3 + 3 = 15

150

Multiplication

Directions: Solve the problems.

9 + 9 = 18
2 nines = 18
2 x 9 = 18

7 + 7 = 14
2 sevens = 14
2 x 7 = 14

Multiplication saves time. It's faster than addition!

4 + 4 + 4 + 4 = 16
4 fours = 16
4 x 4 = 16

8 + 8 + 8 + 8 + 8 = 40
5 eights = 40
5 x 8 = 40

5 + 5 + 5 = 15
3 fives = 15
3 x 5 = 15

9 + 9 = 18
2 nines = 18
2 x 9 = 18

6 + 6 + 6 = 18
3 sixes = 18
3 x 6 = 18

3 + 3 = 6
2 threes = 6
2 x 3 = 6

7 + 7 + 7 + 7 = 28
4 sevens = 28
4 x 7 = 28

2 + 2 = 4
2 twos = 4
2 x 2 = 4

151

Multiplication

Directions: Use the code to color the fish.

If the answer is:

6, color it red.

12, color it orange.

16, color it blue.

27, color it brown.

8, color it yellow.

15, color it green.

18, color it purple.

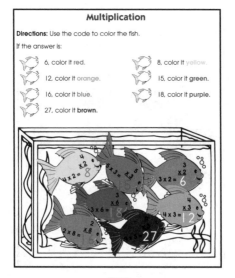

152

Problem Solving

Directions: Tell if you add, subtract, or multiply. Then, write the answers.

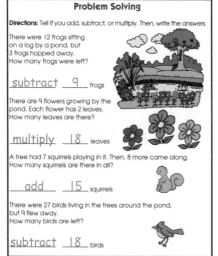

There were 12 frogs sitting on a log by a pond, but 3 frogs hopped away. How many frogs were left?

subtract 9 frogs

There are 9 flowers growing by the pond. Each flower has 2 leaves. How many leaves are there?

multiply 18 leaves

A tree had 7 squirrels playing in it. Then, 8 more came along. How many squirrels are there in all?

add 15 squirrels

There were 27 birds living in the trees around the pond, but 9 flew away. How many birds are left?

subtract 18 birds

153

Answer Key

Circle
A **circle** is a shape that is round. This is a circle: ○

Directions: Find the circles and draw squares around them.

Directions: Trace the word. Then, write the word.

circle   circle

154

Square
A **square** is a shape with four corners and four sides of the same length. This is a square: □

Directions: Find the squares and draw circles around them.

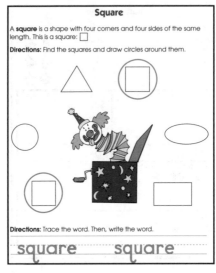

Directions: Trace the word. Then, write the word.

square   square

155

Rectangle
A **rectangle** is a shape with four corners and four sides. The sides opposite each other are the same length. This is a rectangle: ▭

Directions: Find the rectangles and draw circles around them.

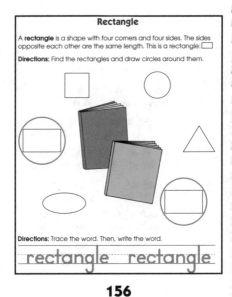

Directions: Trace the word. Then, write the word.

rectangle   rectangle

156

Triangle
A **triangle** is a shape with three corners and three sides. This is a triangle: △

Directions: Find the triangles and draw circles around them.

Directions: Trace the word. Then, write the word.

triangle   triangle

157

Oval and Rhombus
An **oval** is egg-shaped. This is an oval: ○

A **rhombus** is a shape with four sides of the same length. Its corners form points at the top, sides, and bottom. This is a rhombus: ◇

Directions: Find the ovals. Color them red. Find the rhombuses. Color them blue.

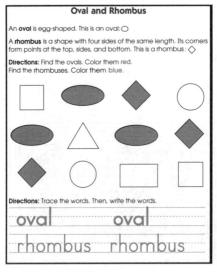

Directions: Trace the words. Then, write the words.

oval   oval
rhombus   rhombus

158

Geometry
Geometry is mathematics that has to do with lines and shapes.

Directions: Color the shapes.

Color the triangles blue.
Color the circles red.
Color the squares green.
Color the rectangles pink.

159

Your Total Solution for Math: Grade 2

Answer Key

Shapes

Directions: Some shapes have sides. How many sides does each shape below have? Write the number of sides inside each shape.

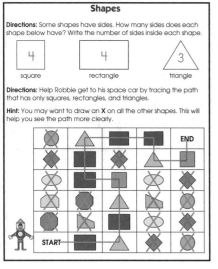

4	4	3
square	rectangle	triangle

Directions: Help Robbie get to his space car by tracing the path that has only squares, rectangles, and triangles.

Hint: You may want to draw an **X** on all the other shapes. This will help you see the path more clearly.

160

Shapes

Directions: Look at the grid below. All the shapes have straight sides, like a square.

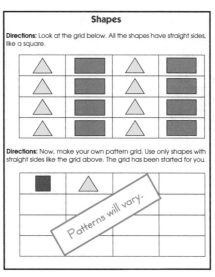

Directions: Now, make your own pattern grid. Use only shapes with straight sides like the grid above. The grid has been started for you.

Patterns will vary.

161

How Big Are You?

Directions: How big are you? **Estimate,** or guess, how long some of your body parts are. Write your estimates below. Then, have a friend use an inch ruler to measure you. Write the numbers below. How close were your estimates?

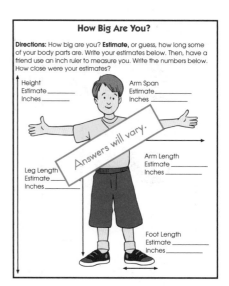

Height Estimate Inches _____

Arm Span Estimate Inches _____

Arm Length Estimate Inches _____

Leg Length Estimate Inches _____

Foot Length Estimate Inches _____

Answers will vary.

162

Measurement: Inches

Directions: Cut out the ruler. Measure each object to the nearest inch.

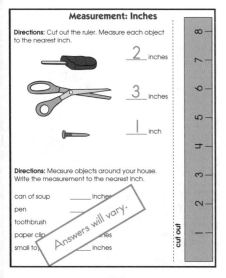

2 inches

3 inches

1 inch

Directions: Measure objects around your house. Write the measurement to the nearest inch.

can of soup _____ inches
pen _____
toothbrush _____
paper clip _____ inches
small to _____ inches

Answers will vary.

cut out

163

Measurement: Inches

Directions: Use the ruler from pg. 163 to measure the fish to the nearest inch.

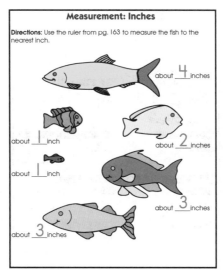

about 4 inches

about 1 inch

about 1 inch

about 2 inches

about 3 inches

about 3 inches

165

Measurement: Inches

An **inch** is a unit of length in the standard measurement system.

Directions: Use the ruler on pg. 163 to measure each object to the nearest inch.

Example: The paper clip is about 1 inch long.

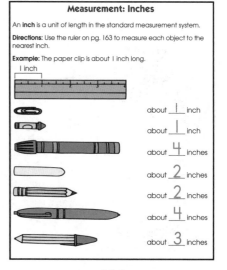

about 1 inch

about 1 inch

about 4 inches

about 2 inches

about 2 inches

about 4 inches

about 3 inches

166

Answer Key

Measuring Monkeys

Directions: Use the inch ruler on pg. 163 to measure the length of each rope. Write the answer in each blank.

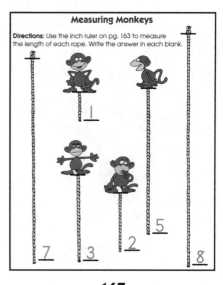

7   3   2   5   8

167

Measurement: Centimeters

A **centimeter** is a unit of length in the metric system. There are 2.54 centimeters in an inch.

Directions: Use a centimeter ruler to measure the crayons to the nearest centimeter.

Example: The first crayon is about 7 centimeters long.

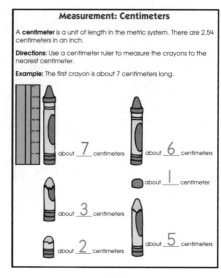

about 7 centimeters   about 6 centimeters

about 1 centimeter

about 3 centimeters

about 2 centimeters   about 5 centimeters

168

Measurement: Centimeters

Directions: The giraffe is about 8 centimeters high. How many centimeters (cm) high are the trees? Write your answers in the blanks.

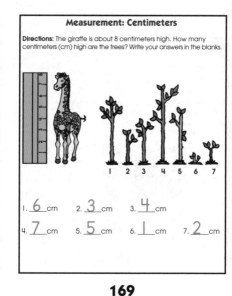

1. 6 cm   2. 3 cm   3. 4 cm

4. 7 cm   5. 5 cm   6. 1 cm   7. 2 cm

169

Trip to the Watering Hole

Directions: Use a centimeter ruler to measure the distance each animal has to travel to reach the watering hole. Write the answer in each blank.

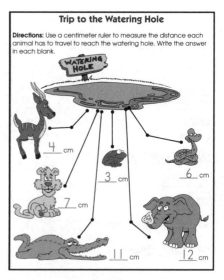

4 cm   3 cm   6 cm   7 cm   11 cm   12 cm

170

Centimeter Sharpening

Directions: Use a centimeter ruler to measure each pencil. Subtract to find how many centimeters were lost when sharpening each pencil.

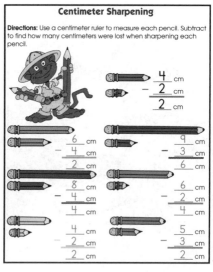

$$\begin{array}{r} 4 \text{ cm} \\ - 2 \text{ cm} \\ \hline 2 \text{ cm} \end{array}$$

$$\begin{array}{r} 6 \text{ cm} \\ - 4 \text{ cm} \\ \hline 2 \text{ cm} \end{array}$$
$$\begin{array}{r} 9 \text{ cm} \\ - 3 \text{ cm} \\ \hline 6 \text{ cm} \end{array}$$

$$\begin{array}{r} 8 \text{ cm} \\ - 4 \text{ cm} \\ \hline 4 \text{ cm} \end{array}$$
$$\begin{array}{r} 6 \text{ cm} \\ - 2 \text{ cm} \\ \hline 4 \text{ cm} \end{array}$$

$$\begin{array}{r} 4 \text{ cm} \\ - 2 \text{ cm} \\ \hline 2 \text{ cm} \end{array}$$
$$\begin{array}{r} 5 \text{ cm} \\ - 3 \text{ cm} \\ \hline 2 \text{ cm} \end{array}$$

171

Good Morning

Directions: Make your own bar graph. List 5 kinds of cereal on the graph below. Ask 5 people to vote for one cereal. Record the votes on the graph by coloring in 1 space for each vote. Use the information to answer the questions.

Favorite Cereal

Cereals

of People

Answers will vary.

1. Which cereal was t_____ _____
2. Which cereal h_____ ___tes?_____
3. How many more ___for _____(name of cereal)_____ than for
_____(name of cereal)_____ ? _____
4. How many people chose _____(name of cereal)_____ and _____(name of cereal)_____ altogether? _____

172

Your Total Solution for Math: Grade 2

Answer Key

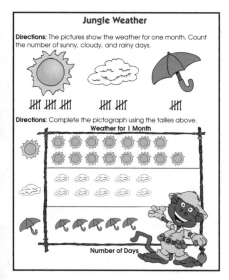

173

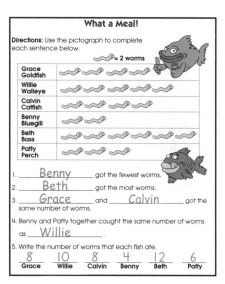

174

"Play Ball"

Directions: Eight baseball teams have just completed their season. Each team played eight games. Use this pictograph to answer the questions below.

1. How many games did the Memphis Monkeys lose? 7
2. Which teams tied for last place?
Lansing Lightning Bugs and Memphis Monkeys
3. Which team won the most games? Jersey Jaguars
4. How many more games did the Washington Wiggle Worms win than the Tampa Toucans? 4
5. Which four teams' total number of games won equal the Jersey Jaguars' number of games won? Kansas City Centipedes, Lansing Lightning Bugs, Houston Hornets, Memphis Monkeys

175

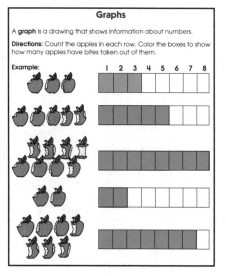

176

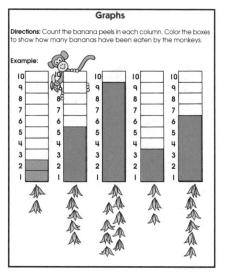

177

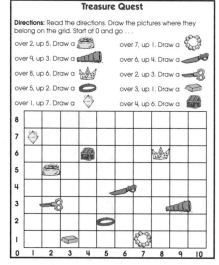

178

Answer Key

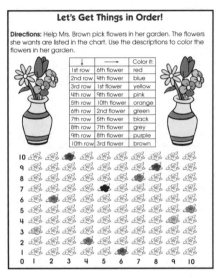

179

180

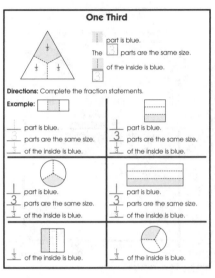

181

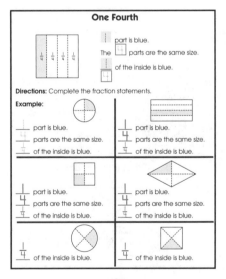

182

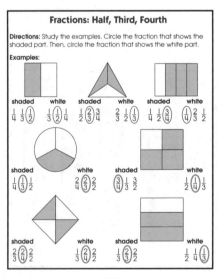

183

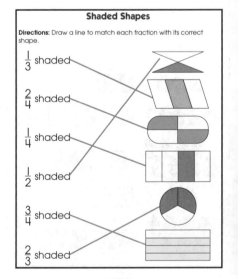

184

Your Total Solution for Math: Grade 2

Answer Key

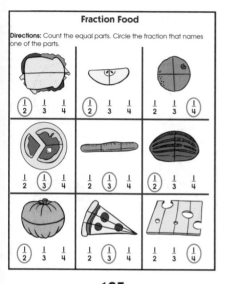

185

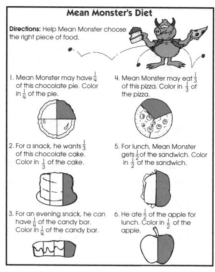

186

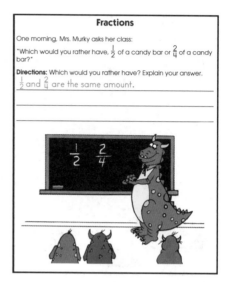

187

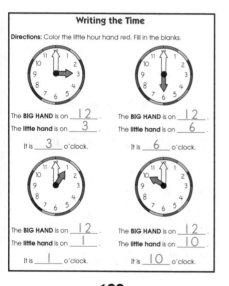

189

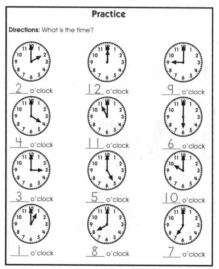

190

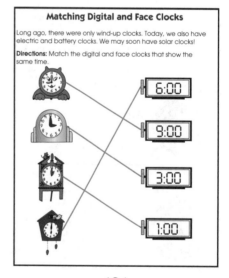

191

Answer Key

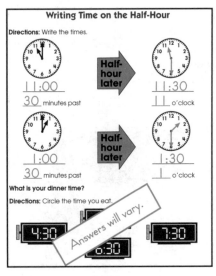

192

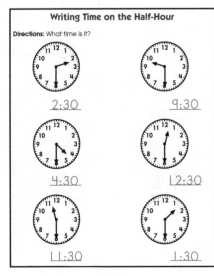

193

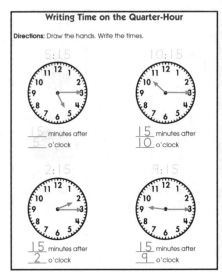

195

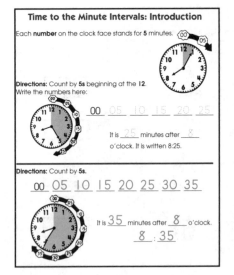

196

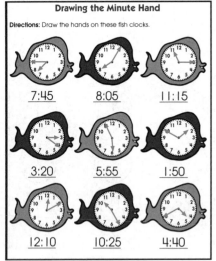

197

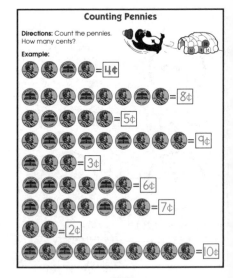

198

Your Total Solution for Math: Grade 2

Answer Key

Counting Pennies

Directions: Count the pennies in each triangle.

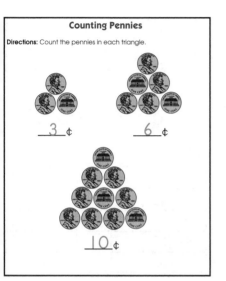

__3__ ¢   __6__ ¢

__10__ ¢

199

Nickels: Introduction

Directions: Look at the two sides of a nickel. Color the nickels silver.

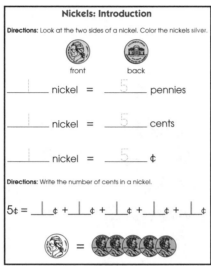

front   back

__1__ nickel = __5__ pennies

__1__ nickel = __5__ cents

__1__ nickel = __5__ ¢

Directions: Write the number of cents in a nickel.

5¢ = __1__ ¢ + __1__ ¢ + __1__ ¢ + __1__ ¢ + __1__ ¢

200

Nickels: Counting by Fives

Directions: Count the nickels by 5s. Write the amount.

Example: 5 cents = 1 nickel

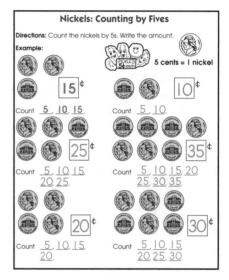

__15__ ¢   __10__ ¢

Count __5, 10, 15__   Count __5, 10__

__25__ ¢   __35__ ¢

Count __5, 10, 15,__   Count __5, 10, 15, 20__
__20, 25__   __25, 30, 35__

__20__ ¢   __30__ ¢

Count __5, 10, 15,__   Count __5, 10, 15__
__20__   __20, 25, 30__

201

Dimes: Introduction

A dime is small, but quite strong. It can buy more than a penny or a nickel.

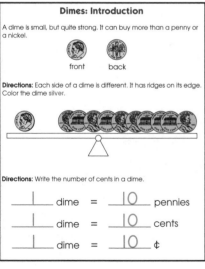

front   back

Directions: Each side of a dime is different. It has ridges on its edge. Color the dime silver.

Directions: Write the number of cents in a dime.

__1__ dime = __10__ pennies

__1__ dime = __10__ cents

__1__ dime = __10__ ¢

202

Dimes: Counting by Tens

Directions: Count by 10s. Write the number. Circle the group with more.

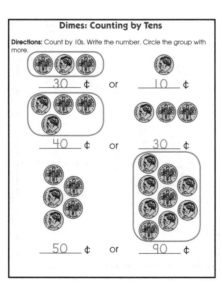

__30__ ¢   or   __10__ ¢

__40__ ¢   or   __30__ ¢

__50__ ¢   or   __90__ ¢

203

Quarters: Introduction

Our first president, George Washington, is on the front. The American eagle is on the back.

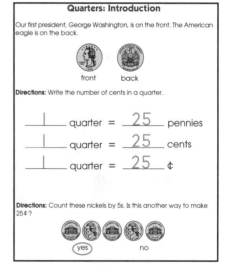

front   back

Directions: Write the number of cents in a quarter.

__1__ quarter = __25__ pennies

__1__ quarter = __25__ cents

__1__ quarter = __25__ ¢

Directions: Count these nickels by 5s. Is this another way to make 25¢?

(yes)   no

204

Answer Key

Counting With Quarters

These are some machines that use quarters.

Directions: Color each machine you have to put quarters into. Circle the number of quarters you need.

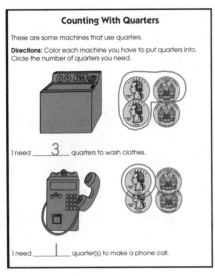

I need ___3___ quarters to wash clothes.

I need ___1___ quarter(s) to make a phone call.

205

Counting With Quarters, Dimes, Nickels, and Pennies

Directions: Match the money with the amount.

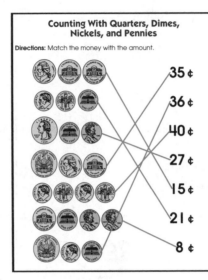

35 ¢

36 ¢

40 ¢

27 ¢

15 ¢

21 ¢

8 ¢

206

Counting With Quarters, Dimes, Nickels, and Pennies

Here are things to buy for your hair.

Directions: How many of each coin do you need? Write 1, 2, 3, or 4.

	Quarters	Dimes	Nickels	Pennies
			1	2
	1	1		4
	1			4
			1	3
		2		

207

Subtracting for Change

Adam wanted to know how much change he would have left when he bought things. He made this picture to help him subtract.

```
  4 dimes          40 ¢
- 1 dime         - 10 ¢
  3 dimes          30 ¢
```

Directions: Cross out and subtract.

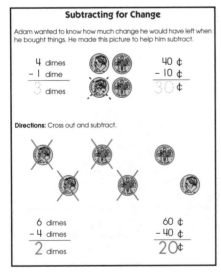

```
  6 dimes          60 ¢
- 4 dimes        - 40 ¢
  2 dimes          20 ¢
```

208

Problem-Solving with Money

Directions: Draw the coins you use. Write the number of coins on each blank.

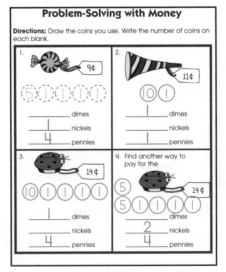

1. 9¢
___ dimes
___ nickels
4 pennies

2. 11¢
1 dimes
___ nickels
1 pennies

3. 14¢
1 dimes
___ nickels
4 pennies

4. Find another way to pay for the
___ dimes
2 nickels
4 pennies

209

Making Exact Amounts of Money: Two Ways to Pay

Directions: Find two ways to pay. Show what coins you use.

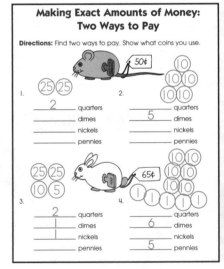

1. 50¢
2 quarters
___ dimes
___ nickels
___ pennies

2.
___ quarters
5 dimes
___ nickels
___ pennies

3. 65¢
2 quarters
1 dimes
___ nickels
___ pennies

4.
___ quarters
6 dimes
___ nickels
5 pennies

210

Answer Key

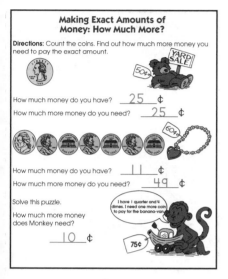

Making Exact Amounts of Money: How Much More?

Directions: Count the coins. Find out how much more money you need to pay the exact amount.

How much money do you have? __25__ ¢
How much more money do you need? __25__ ¢

How much money do you have? __11__ ¢
How much more money do you need? __49__ ¢

Solve this puzzle.

How much more money does Monkey need?

__10__ ¢

211

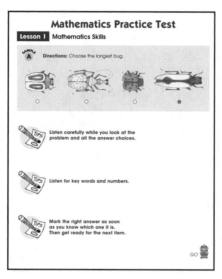

Mathematics Practice Test

Lesson 1 Mathematics Skills

SAMPLE A **Directions:** Choose the longest bug.

TIPS — Listen carefully while you look at the problem and all the answer choices.

TIPS — Listen for key words and numbers.

TIPS — Mark the right answer as soon as you know which one it is. Then get ready for the next item.

GO

214

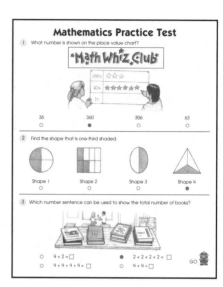

Mathematics Practice Test

1. What number is shown on the place value chart?

36 ○   360 ●   306 ○   63 ○

2. Find the shape that is one-third shaded.

Shape 1 ○   Shape 2 ○   Shape 3 ○   Shape 4 ●

3. Which number sentence can be used to show the total number of books?

○ 4 + 2 = □   ● 2 + 2 + 2 + 2 = □
○ 4 + 4 + 4 = □   ○ 4 + 4 = □

GO

215

Mathematics Practice Test

4. Which tool would students use to measure a pint of water from the stream?

hanging scale ○   tape measure ○   measuring cup ●   thermometer ○

5. Pablo has two quarters, one dime, and three nickels. How much money does he have in all?

75¢ ○   65¢ ●   60¢ ○   70¢ ○

GO

216

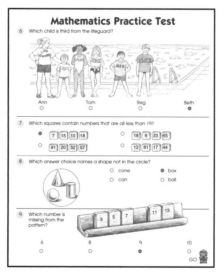

Mathematics Practice Test

6. Which child is third from the lifeguard?

Ann ○   Tom ○   Reg ○   Beth ●

7. Which squares contain numbers that are all less than 19?

● 7 15 10 18   ○ 18 6 23 65
○ 91 20 32 57   ○ 12 81 17 44

8. Which answer choice names a shape not in the circle?

○ cone   ● box
○ can   ○ ball

9. Which number is missing from the pattern?

6 ○   8 ●   9 ○   10 ○

GO

217

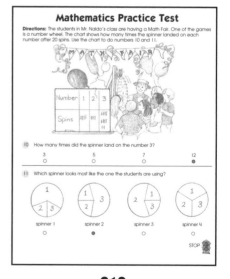

Mathematics Practice Test

Directions: The students in Mr. Naldo's class are having a Math Fair. One of the games is a number wheel. The chart shows how many times the spinner landed on each number after 20 spins. Use the chart to do numbers 10 and 11.

10. How many times did the spinner land on the number 3?

3 ○   5 ○   7 ○   12 ●

11. Which spinner looks most like the one the students are using?

spinner 1 ○   spinner 2 ●   spinner 3 ○   spinner 4 ○

STOP

218

Answer Key

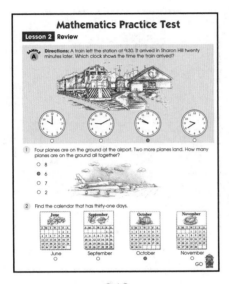

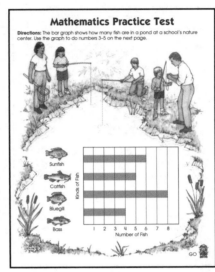

219   220   221

Your Total Solution for Math: Grade 2